HOLT

Elements of
Language

FIFTH COURSE

Chapter Tests

- Reading
- Writing
- Sentences and Paragraphs
- Grammar, Usage, Mechanics

HOLT, RINEHART AND WINSTON

A Harcourt Education Company

Orlando • Austin • New York • San Diego • London

ISBN 978-0-03-099149-3

ISBN 0-03-099149-8

2 3 4 5 6   018   13 12 11 10 09 08

Table of Contents

Table of Contents

Communications

About These Tests

Every chapter in your *Elements of Language* Student Edition has an accompanying Chapter Test in traditional format. The Answer Keys for these tests are located on the *Teacher One Stop*.

Part 1 **Grammar, Usage, and Mechanics**

The Part 1 tests provide assessment for the rules and key concepts taught in the grammar, usage, and mechanics chapters in the Student Edition. Students demonstrate their mastery of the instruction by completing a variety of tests that are similar to the exercises in the Student Edition.

Part 2 **Sentences and Paragraphs**

The Part 2 tests provide assessment for each major section within the Sentences and Paragraphs chapters. Students complete exercises similar to those in the Student Edition. These exercises test students' mastery of the key concepts taught in the chapters.

Part 3 **Communications**

The Part 3 tests include assessment for both the Reading and the Writing Workshops. You may choose to administer the Reading and Writing Workshop tests separately or as one test after students have completed the chapter.

In the **Reading Workshop** test, students read a passage, respond to short-answer questions, and complete a graphic organizer. The passage is in the mode that students have just studied, and the questions and the graphic organizer assess students' proficiency in the chapter's Reading Skill and Reading Focus.

The **Writing Workshop** test provides a passage containing problems or errors in several or all of the following areas: content, organization, style, grammar and usage, and mechanics. Students demonstrate their understanding of the mode of writing and their revising and proofreading skills by revising the essay and correcting the errors. A Revising Guidelines page reminds students of the chapter skills and the basic requirements of the chapter writing mode.

To help students complete the Writing Workshop tests, you may want to give them photocopies of the following page, which lists symbols for revising and proofreading.

Symbols for Revising and Proofreading

The following symbols will help you revise and correct the passages in the Writing Workshop tests.

SYMBOL	DEFINITION	EXAMPLE
ℰ	Delete word.	The girl smiled ~~at me.~~ ℰ
∧	Insert.	The girl smiled. ^{at me} ∧
∧—	Replace a word.	I found the ^{record} ~~book.~~
≡	Set in capital letters.	Does karen like fish?
/	Set in lowercase.	Does Karen Łike Ƒish?
✓	Insert apostrophe.	Its his dog.
❝❞	Insert quotation marks.	It's his dog, he said.
⊙	Insert period.	If she goes, I go⊙
∧	Insert comma.	If she goes I go.
⊙	Insert colon.	Pick a color: red, blue, or green.
⌃	Insert semicolon.	We went; she stayed.

Parts of Speech Overview: Identification and Function

A. CLASSIFYING NOUNS Classify the italicized noun in each of the following sentences by writing above it *common*, *proper*, *collective*, or *compound*. Some nouns have more than one classification.

Example 1. Learning to play the guitar also taught me *self-discipline*. [*common, compound* written above *self-discipline*]

1. In the 1500s Tenochtitlán, the capital of the Aztec Empire, was larger than any city in *Spain*.

2. The *crowd* of holiday shoppers filled the aisles of the toy store.

3. Found abandoned at the *airport*, the stolen car was returned to its owner.

4. For *dessert* Todd served a delicious pumpkin pie.

5. The *Declaration of Independence* was adopted on July 4, 1776.

B. IDENTIFYING PRONOUNS Underline each pronoun in the following sentences.

Example 1. We hope you will visit us in our new home.

6. This calculator is yours; do you know who has mine?

7. If I may have your attention, please, we can begin our program without further delay.

8. Jerome reminded himself not to forget his grandmother's birthday.

9. All of us wished Ms. Golden a safe journey as she left on her vacation.

10. Do any of you know anything about the Iroquois and their confederation?

11. This is the week when each of our teachers will review the portfolios that we have assembled.

12. I think something is missing from this chili that you made; its flavor is too bland.

13. Did your shift supervisor recommend you for the position herself?

14. Even those who have studied English before coming to the United States may find some American idioms puzzling.

15. Those of us who are reading Robert Frost's poetry discussed his use of deceptively simple language.

C. IDENTIFYING ADJECTIVES AND ADVERBS Underline each italicized adjective in the following sentences once, and underline each italicized adverb twice.

Example 1. Are you *familiar* with the works of the sculptor who uses *only* the name Marisol?

16. Marisol Escobar was born in 1930 to a *Venezuelan* couple *then* living in Paris.

17. *Today* she is *quite* well known throughout the world.

18. Carved from wood, her *clever, life-sized* figures fascinate both children and adults.

19. Marisol gives *each* figure a *unique* personality by drawing or painting a face on it.

20. She *often* adds other *real-life* touches, such as clothing.

21. To some of the figures, she *even* adds *plaster* casts of her hands, feet, or face.

22. Many of Marisol's sculptures represent people who exist *solely* in her *extraordinary* imagination.

23. *Sometimes*, though, she portrays *actual* people.

24. One of her *best-known* works is called *simply* <u>The Family</u>.

25. Wouldn't it be fun to have a *Marisol* sculpture of your *own* family?

D. IDENTIFYING AND CLASSIFYING VERBS AND VERB PHRASES Underline the verbs and verb phrases in the following sentences. Then, on the line provided, classify each verb or verb phrase as a *transitive action verb, intransitive action verb,* or *linking verb.* Use these abbreviations: *TRANS* for *transitive action verb, INT* for *intransitive action verb,* and *LINK* for *linking verb.*

Example *TRANS* **1.** I will <u>meet</u> you at the food court in an hour.

_____ **26.** Who sounded the alarm?

_____ **27.** Your idea sounds practical to me.

_____ **28.** Palani must have left without us.

_____ **29.** For our trip to Boston in January, we will pack our warmest clothes.

_____ **30.** Please stand for our national anthem.

E. IDENTIFYING THE PARTS OF SPEECH On the line provided, identify each italicized word in the following sentences as a *noun,* a *pronoun,* an *adjective,* a *verb,* an *adverb,* a *preposition,* a *conjunction,* or an *interjection.* Use these abbreviations:

N for *noun*	ADV for *adverb*
PRO for *pronoun*	PREP for *preposition*
ADJ for *adjective*	CONJ for *conjunction*
V for *verb*	INT for *interjection*

Example _✓_ **1.** Are you among those who *harbor* a secret ambition?

_____ **31.** *Several* of my friends have confided their secret ambitions to me.

_____ **32.** As a loyal friend, I respect their *privacy*.

_____ **33.** Therefore, they will remain *nameless* in this account.

_____ **34.** In any case, their identities are *less* important than their aspirations.

_____ **35.** One friend *longs* to climb Mount Everest.

_____ **36.** Another dreams of staging a one-woman show before a *Broadway* audience.

_____ **37.** A *third* imagines himself as the White House chief of staff.

_____ **38.** I could go *on*, but you get the idea.

_____ **39.** *Do* any of these dreams strike a responsive chord in you?

_____ **40.** I *too* have my dreams.

_____ **41.** Sometimes I picture *myself* conducting the Chicago Symphony Orchestra.

_____ **42.** At other times, I mentally rehearse my speech *before* a distinguished audience in Stockholm.

_____ **43.** *What*, you wonder, is the occasion?

_____ **44.** *Well*, you see, I am accepting the Nobel Prize in literature.

_____ **45.** *Although* you may laugh, my friends and I cherish such dreams.

_____ **46.** We realize that making dreams *like* these come true will require hard work.

_____ **47.** That prospect does *not* discourage us, however.

_____ **48.** In *fact*, we view it as a challenge.

_____ **49.** How far will our dreams *and* hard work take us?

_____ **50.** *Only* time will tell.

The Parts of a Sentence: Subjects, Predicates, Complements

A. IDENTIFYING SENTENCES AND SENTENCE FRAGMENTS On the line provided, identify each of the following word groups as either a sentence or a sentence fragment. Write *S* for *sentence* or *F* for *fragment*.

Example ___F___ **1.** When the next train leaves for Pittsburgh.

_____ **1.** Where the Allegheny River and the Monongahela River come together to form the Ohio River.

_____ **2.** In the seventeenth century, the original group of American Indians in the area were supplanted by Iroquois from western New York.

_____ **3.** Settlers from Britain and France tried to claim the land during the following century.

_____ **4.** The conflict between the two nations, the French and Indian War, which lasted from 1754 to 1763.

_____ **5.** Pittsburgh grew up around a British fort named for William Pitt.

_____ **6.** Then Britain's secretary of state and a champion of the colonists' rights.

_____ **7.** In the nineteenth century, called Steel City because it produced more steel than anywhere else in the world.

_____ **8.** Pittsburgh is no longer dependent on a single industry.

_____ **9.** Offers many varied cultural opportunities such as the Pittsburgh Symphony Orchestra at Heinz Hall for the Performing Arts where we are going to a concert this evening.

_____ **10.** What a great time we'll have!

B. IDENTIFYING SUBJECTS AND VERBS For each of the following sentences, underline the simple subject once and the verb twice. Be sure to include all parts of a compound subject or a compound verb and all words in a verb phrase. If the subject is understood to be *you*, write (*you*) on the line provided.

Example _(you)_ **1.** Please take a number and wait in line.

_____ **11.** Both the teacher and the students enjoyed the field trip to the state capitol.

_____ **12.** There will be a brief delay before takeoff.

_____ **13.** Did you see any of your friends at the mall?

_____ **14.** Here in New Hampshire, our motto is "Live Free or Die."

_____ **15.** In addition to the enchiladas, please bring guacamole and sliced tomatoes.

_____ **16.** The board of directors met on Thursday afternoon and approved the merger.

_____ **17.** The plates, serving bowls, and silverware can go into the dishwasher.

_____ **18.** This album of Irish songs is always a big hit at St. Patrick's Day parties.

_____ **19.** Parts of Argentina, Bolivia, Chile, Colombia, Ecuador, and Peru were once ruled by

the Inca.

_____ **20.** Your essay has been accepted for publication and will appear in our May issue.

C. IDENTIFYING COMPLEMENTS On the line provided, identify the italicized complement or complements in each of the following sentences. Use these abbreviations:

      DO for *direct object*   *IO* for *indirect object*   *OC* for *objective complement*

      PN for *predicate nominative*   *PA* for *predicate adjective*

Example __*IO*__ **1.** The coach hit *us* flies and grounders for fielding practice this afternoon.

_____ **21.** The President will hold a *press conference* this afternoon at 3:00 P.M.

_____ **22.** A section of the Pennsylvania Turnpike was the first *freeway* in the United States.

_____ **23.** We named the puppies that we adopted from the animal shelter *Sugar* and *Spice*.

_____ **24.** Your idea doesn't seem *silly* to me.

_____ **25.** Grandpa Jefferson's visit made the holiday *memorable*.

_____ **26.** What an *eyesore* our neighbor's front yard is!

_____ **27.** Has Anita found the *ring* that she lost last week?

_____ **28.** Please leave *me* a phone number where I can reach you this evening.

_____ **29.** The audience clearly found the play *entertaining*.

_____ **30.** Who is *responsible* for the mess in the basement?

_____ **31.** The painting that won the blue ribbon was an abstract *self-portrait*.

_____ **32.** How *thoughtful* you were to remember my birthday.

_____ **33.** As the crowd looked on admiringly, Tiger Woods sank the *putt* to finish the round.

_____ **34.** What are the seniors giving the *school* as a class present?

_____ **35.** Patsy T. Mink of Hawaii first became a *member* of the U.S. Congress in 1965.

_____ **36.** How many *colleges* have you visited so far?

_____ **37.** According to weather forecasters, an end to the drought appears *unlikely* any time soon.

_____ **38.** We never give our *dog* Barney any small bones or chocolate.

_____ **39.** The tired toddler threw a *tantrum* at the grocery store.

_____ **40.** Most of the people in the article on longevity were *nonagenarians* or *centenarians*.

D. IDENTIFYING SENTENCES ACCORDING TO PURPOSE On the line provided, identify each of the following sentences as declarative, interrogative, imperative, or exclamatory. Use these abbreviations: *DEC* for *declarative*, *INT* for *interrogative*, *IMP* for *imperative*, and *EXC* for *exclamatory*. Then, add an appropriate end mark for each sentence.

Example _DEC_ **1.** The neighborhood was built in an area that had once been swampland.

_____ **41.** How handsome you look in your new suit

_____ **42.** We rode more than twenty miles on our bicycles last weekend, and we have the sore muscles to prove it

_____ **43.** Where the road forks, bear left and go to the third stoplight

_____ **44.** What a disaster our dress rehearsal last night was

_____ **45.** Have you seen my electronic organizer around here anywhere

_____ **46.** Try not to let your part-time job interfere with your studies

_____ **47.** Soccer practice was canceled today because a tornado watch was issued in mid-afternoon

_____ **48.** If you have time, send me a postcard while you are on vacation

_____ **49.** When is the Supreme Court scheduled to hear the appeal

_____ **50.** Under the fence squirmed the next-door neighbor's dog

The Phrase: Kinds of Phrases and Their Functions

A. IDENTIFYING PREPOSITIONAL PHRASES   Identify each prepositional phrase in the following sentences by underlining *adjective phrases* once and *adverb phrases* twice.

Example   1. In the United States, the first Monday in September is celebrated as Labor Day.

1. The weather in this area has usually turned bitterly cold by January.

2. Did you get a chance after school yesterday to read my essay on cheerleading?

3. None of us will have time for many outside activities during finals week.

4. The sequel is similar to the original movie in plot but quite different from it otherwise.

5. The backup along the interstate lasted throughout the morning because of the fog and drizzle.

6. On graduation night, the city sponsors a huge party at the Midtown Civic Center for seniors and their dates.

7. Have you ever thought about spending a year in another country as an exchange student?

8. Over spring vacation we will visit the Mexican state of Puebla, which lies between Mexico City and the Gulf of Mexico.

9. Mom wasn't able to get home before six Friday night, so we didn't leave town until almost an hour after breakfast the next morning.

10. Please fold the grocery bags and put them inside the cabinet next to the refrigerator.

B. IDENTIFYING VERBAL PHRASES   Underline each *participial phrase* in the following sentences once and each *gerund phrase* twice. Circle each infinitive phrase.

Example   1. The coach plans to fine-tune the game plan before the playoffs.

11. Boarding *Air Force One*, the President paused briefly and waved to the crowd.

12. Did you manage to complete your project for the science fair by the deadline?

13. Corazon devotes some of her spare time to making deliveries for the Meals on Wheels program.

14. I am looking for a gift to give my grandmother on her birthday.

15. Serving as a mentor for a fourth-grader this year has been both challenging and rewarding.

16. The experience has reinforced my desire to become a teacher.

17. Felix, searching for a part-time job, has filled out nearly two dozen applications.

18. One of our neighbors is raising a puppy that will be trained to serve as a guide dog for a person with a visual impairment.

19. What gave me the most difficulty at first when I was driving was paying such close attention to what I was doing.

20. The tulip bulbs planted around the mailbox should be blooming soon.

C. IDENTIFYING APPOSITIVE PHRASES   Underline each appositive phrase in the following sentences.

Example 1. A hand-me-down from my sister, the computer suits me just fine.

21. Our nation's first President, George Washington, was inaugurated on April 30, 1789.

22. Are you familiar with the works of Gabriela Mistral, the Chilean poet who won the Nobel Prize for literature in 1945?

23. A souvenir of our trip to Hawaii, this menu describes the delicious food that we were served at a luau.

24. My stepbrother's favorite public radio program, *All Things Considered*, airs Monday through Friday every week.

25. An internationally known motion picture star, Denzel Washington began his career as a stage actor in New York City.

26. Have you met Uncle Gary, my mom's older brother?

27. Proud new citizens of the United States, my aunt and uncle posed for pictures in front of the Statue of Liberty.

28. The cat, an orange tabby, looked as if it had not eaten in days.

29. Birds of prey, owls eat other birds as well as small mammals and reptiles.

30. How many New Yorkers do you suppose have visited their state's capital, Albany?

D. IDENTIFYING PREPOSITIONAL, VERBAL, AND APPOSITIVE PHRASES   On the line provided, identify the kind of phrase that is italicized in each of the following sentences. Use these abbreviations: *PREP* for *prepositional phrase*, *PART* for *participial phrase*, *GER* for *gerund phrase*, *INF* for *infinitive phrase*, and *APP* for *appositive phrase*. Do not separately identify a prepositional phrase or a verbal phrase that is part of another phrase.

Example _PART_ **1.** *Invigorated by our brisk walk,* we resumed our study session.

_____ **31.** *Interviewing an expert* is one good way to gather information on a topic.

_____ **32.** The lamp, a sale item, was just what I had in mind *for Uncle John and Aunt Susan's anniversary gift.*

_____ **33.** The student council has drafted a proposal *to present to the principal.*

_____ **34.** Unfortunately, the game had to be stopped *because of the high wind and rain.*

_____ **35.** In many of his works, Pulitzer Prize winner *N. Scott Momaday* explores his Native American heritage.

_____ **36.** One of my family's favorite pastimes is *playing touch football.*

_____ **37.** The governor's plans *for privatizing several state services* have drawn strong opposition.

_____ **38.** I have decided *to wait here.*

_____ **39.** Along the shores of the stream grow scores of wildflowers *nourished by the rich alluvial soil.*

_____ **40.** Your opinion seems unsupportable *to me.*

_____ **41.** Langston Hughes, *a leading figure in the Harlem Renaissance,* is the subject of a two-volume biography by Arnold Rampersad.

_____ **42.** Mathematicians in ancient China were apparently the earliest *to explore the value of pi.*

_____ **43.** *The ratio of a circle's circumference to its diameter,* pi is constant for every circle.

_____ **44.** *To replace the ceramic tile in the bathroom* is Mom's next project.

_____ **45.** Nancy Lopez did a great deal *to popularize women's professional golf.*

_____ **46.** What is that bird *circling overhead*?

_____ **47.** *Nestled between the mountains and the sea,* the village offers spectacular vistas in every direction.

_____ **48.** Your *longing for a break in this rainy weather* is shared by many people.

_____ **49.** Granddad, I'd like you to meet Mrs. Davenport, *my history teacher.*

_____ **50.** *Having finished my first half-marathon,* I was exhausted but jubilant.

The Clause: Independent and Subordinate Clauses

A. IDENTIFYING INDEPENDENT AND SUBORDINATE CLAUSES On the line provided, identify the italicized word group in each of the following sentences as an independent clause or a subordinate clause. Write *IND* for *independent clause* and *SUB* for *subordinate clause*.

Example _SUB_ **1.** *Where to find a part-time job* is Lee's most pressing concern right now.

_____ **1.** Rita Dove, *who was born in Akron, Ohio, in 1952,* was our nation's poet laureate from 1993 to 1995.

_____ **2.** Not *until I was twelve years old* did my family have a computer.

_____ **3.** *The holiday* that I enjoy most *is Thanksgiving.*

_____ **4.** The manufacturer's claim is *that the product is completely safe and effective.*

_____ **5.** When a piece of red litmus paper is exposed to a base, *the paper turns blue.*

_____ **6.** *Martin Luther King, Jr., was only fifteen* when he entered Morehouse College in Atlanta.

_____ **7.** The family *to whom the package is addressed* no longer lives in this apartment complex.

_____ **8.** *Who the people in this picture are* is a mystery to all of us.

_____ **9.** *How surprised we were* when the parrot alighted on our balcony.

_____ **10.** Hand *whoever passes by* one of these fliers about today's pep rally.

B. IDENTIFYING ADJECTIVE CLAUSES AND THE WORDS THEY MODIFY Underline the adjective clause in each of the following sentences, and circle the noun or pronoun that the clause modifies. Then, on the line provided, identify the relative pronoun in the adjective clause as a subject, a direct object, or an object of a preposition. If the adjective clause has no relative pronoun, write *None*. Use these abbreviations: *S* for *subject*, *DO* for *direct object*, and *OP* for *object of a preposition*.

Example _OP_ **1.** The (teacher) for whom Mr. Munoz is substituting today is Ms. Dorsey.

_____ **11.** My last class of the day, which is Latin III, is one of my favorites.

_____ **12.** Ms. Dorsey, who usually teaches our class, is away at a teachers' convention.

_____ **13.** I think that she is the best teacher I have ever had.

_____ **14.** Although Latin III is a hard course in which we usually have homework and at least one quiz or test a week, she somehow makes the class enjoyable.

_____ **15.** This month we are reading selections by Cicero, who lived from 106 to 43 B.C.

_____ **16.** Cicero was a Roman writer whom scholars credit with introducing important Greek ideas to Rome.

_____ **17.** For centuries, his prose has served as a model that aspiring writers have studied.

_____ **18.** Some friends who are taking other languages tease me about studying a "dead" one.

_____ **19.** I counter with a little-known fact that I learned from Ms. Dorsey.

_____ **20.** As many as half the words they commonly use are derived from this "dead" language.

C. IDENTIFYING NOUN CLAUSES Underline the noun clause in each of the following sentences. On the line provided, identify how the noun clause is used in the sentence. Use these abbreviations: *S* for *subject*, *PN* for *predicate nominative*, *DO* for *direct object*, *IO* for *indirect object*, and *OP* for *object of a preposition*.

Example ___*IO*___ **1.** Police officers will give <u>whoever blocks the fire lanes</u> a ticket.

_____ **21.** That the deadline for the essay contest is April 15 was announced months ago.

_____ **22.** The detour on Archer Avenue was what made us late for my cousin's wedding.

_____ **23.** Did your parents suggest that you cut back on your hours at work?

_____ **24.** Please give whoever asks for it my new address.

_____ **25.** Of course I remember when your birthday is.

_____ **26.** Be sure to express your appreciation once in a while to whomever you consider your role model.

_____ **27.** How the media are converging is the newsmagazine's cover story this week.

_____ **28.** The reporter asked the mayor about what she planned to cover in her speech.

_____ **29.** The mayor replied that she owes all her success to her family.

_____ **30.** Whoever the anonymous donor is certainly has our deepest gratitude.

D. IDENTIFYING ADVERB CLAUSES AND THE WORDS THEY MODIFY Underline the adverb clause in each of the following sentences, and circle the word or words that the clause modifies. Then, on the line provided, identify whether the clause tells *how, when, where, why, to what extent,* or *under what condition.*

Example ___*to what extent*___ **1.** My schedule is (busier) now <u>than it was last year.</u>

_____ **31.** You look as though you could use a study break.

_____ **32.** Thrilled because he had made the Honor Society, Eric e-mailed his aunt.

_____ **33.** I will call you if I am going to be late for the meeting.

_____ **34.** When Ellen Taaffe Zwilich won the Pulitzer Prize in music in 1983, she became the first woman so honored.

_____ **35.** You are exactly three months younger than I am.

_____ **36.** Most schools require that students have certain vaccinations so that infectious diseases are not spread throughout the school population.

_____ **37.** I often listen to music on my headphones while I clean my room.

_____ **38.** Once finals are over, we can all relax.

_____ **39.** Last night we played basketball at the park until we could no longer

see the backboard.

_____ **40.** I will not finish my report on the Iroquois League tonight unless I can

get to the library this afternoon.

E. CLASSIFYING SENTENCES BY STRUCTURE On the line provided, classify each of the following
sentences according to its structure. Use these abbreviations: *S* for *simple*, *CD* for *compound*, *CX* for
complex, and *CD-CX* for *compound-complex*.

Example __CX__ **1.** When we go to Mexico next summer, we will visit Mexico City and tour the

Tamayo Museum of Contemporary International Art.

_____ **41.** The museum is named for Mexican painter Rufino Tamayo, whose work I have

admired in books and magazines.

_____ **42.** Tamayo's paintings may not be as well known in this country as those of his compa-

triot Diego Rivera, but they are highly regarded by many art critics.

_____ **43.** I am hoping to see some of Tamayo's works in person, and, if prints of them are avail-

able, I plan to buy at least one for my room.

_____ **44.** Tamayo was born in 1899 in Oaxaca, which is a state in the southern part of Mexico.

_____ **45.** In his early twenties, he went to work for the National Museum of Anthropology in

Mexico City.

_____ **46.** His duties there provided him with the opportunities to study and sketch examples of

pre-Columbian Indian sculpture.

_____ **47.** During the course of their careers, many great artists experiment with a number of

different styles, and Tamayo was no exception.

_____ **48.** His familiarity with modern European art movements is evident in his work as early

as the 1930s.

_____ **49.** As he grew older, he became increasingly interested in using nonrepresentational art to

express his views on the meaning of life.

_____ **50.** When Rufino Tamayo died in 1991, his place in art history was secure, for he is consid-

ered one of Mexico's most important twentieth-century painters.

Agreement: Subject and Verb, Pronoun and Antecedent

A. IDENTIFYING CORRECT SUBJECT-VERB AGREEMENT Underline the correct word or word group in parentheses in each of the following sentences.

Example 1. Many of the questions on the test (*was, were*) multiple-choice items.

1. On a regulation baseball field, ninety feet (*is, are*) the distance between the bases.

2. Maria, together with Frank and Matthew, (*is, are*) planning to audition for parts in the next school play.

3. I missed the speaker's closing words because someone a few rows ahead (*was, were*) coughing uncontrollably.

4. The sponsors will give everyone who (*registers, register*) for the race a T-shirt.

5. Several of the stores in the mall (*offers, offer*) discount cards to frequent shoppers.

6. Watering the flowers in the window boxes (*is, are*) one of my little sister's chores.

7. Where (*is, are*) the scissors, Mom?

8. Neither the forecasters at the National Weather Service nor the meteorologist on my favorite local television station (*was, were*) right about the path of the storm.

9. In how many different ways (*has, have*) electronics changed our everyday lives in just the past decade?

10. My friend and classmate Carlos often (*gives, give*) me a ride to school.

11. A swarm of bees (*has, have*) taken up residence in the park's gazebo.

12. The number of bees in the swarm (*is, are*) estimated at several thousand.

13. (*Has, Have*) all of the leftover turkey been eaten already?

14. Neither of my brothers (*is, are*) what you would call a sports fanatic.

15. *American Dragons: Twenty-five Asian American Voices* (*was, were*) compiled by Laurence Yep and published by HarperCollins.

16. On the front page of this morning's newspaper (*is, are*) pictures of last night's fire in the warehouse district.

17. The speed limit in our neighborhood (*is, are*) fifteen miles an hour.

18. (*Don't, Doesn't*) anyone have change for a dollar?

19. Every table and booth (*was, were*) taken by the time we reached the restaurant.

20. Four score and seven years (*equals, equal*) eighty-seven years.

B. IDENTIFYING CORRECT PRONOUN-ANTECEDENT AGREEMENT   Underline the correct word or word group in parentheses in each of the following sentences.

Example 1. Either Dorothy or Mavis will present (*her, their*) speech this afternoon.

21. The committee managed to discuss all of the items on (*its, their*) agenda in just two hours.

22. All of the candidates promised not to use negative advertising in (*his or her, their*) campaigns.

23. On Saturday Uncle Max and Aunt Polly showed us movies of (*his or her, their*) trip to Spain.

24. Neither Sean nor Joel failed any of (*his, their*) courses last year.

25. Each of the girls stated (*her, their*) position on the issue.

26. Before each game, the Trueville Tigers gather around (*its, their*) coach for a pep talk.

27. The emphasis on athletics at that university has been criticized lately, but (*it, they*) will bring in a large share of the university's revenue again this year.

28. Someone in our neighborhood has been using (*his or her, their*) noisy power tools too early in the morning the past couple of weekends.

29. The macaroni and cheese will be ready to serve as soon as I finish stirring (*it, them*).

30. Most of the meeting went smoothly, and (*it, they*) adjourned promptly at nine o'clock.

C. PROOFREADING FOR SUBJECT-VERB AND PRONOUN-ANTECEDENT AGREEMENT   Most of the following sentences contain at least one error in subject-verb or pronoun-antecedent agreement. Draw a line through the incorrect verb or pronoun and write the correct form above it. If the sentence is already correct, write *C* on the line provided.

Example _____ **1.** The kind of music I like best ~~are~~ *is* the blues, which ~~are~~ *is* truly an American art form.

_____ **31.** Edward Kennedy "Duke" Ellington is one of the composers who are highly esteemed by jazz fans.

_____ **32.** Anyone who knows anything about jazz recognize Ellington's name.

_____ **33.** The composer and arranger was born in Washington, D.C., in 1899 and began playing the piano when he was only seven years old.

_____ **34.** Most of us who enjoys jazz are able to name half a dozen or more of his works.

_____ **35.** Among my favorite compositions by Ellington is "Mood Indigo" and "Sophisticated Lady."

_____ **36.** *Black, Brown, and Beige*, written in 1943, are one of Ellington's longer works.

_____ **37.** Does any of those titles ring a bell with you?

      ELEMENTS OF LANGUAGE | Fifth Course

_____ **38.** The title of another of Ellington's compositions are credited with being the source of the name *swing music*.

_____ **39.** That title, "It Don't Mean a Thing If It Ain't Got That Swing," certainly don't follow the guidelines of standard English usage.

_____ **40.** Yet it, as well as the song's tune, certainly are catchy.

_____ **41.** Ellington wrote many of his most popular songs between the mid-1930's and mid-1940's; in fact, those are considered his most creative period.

_____ **42.** "Take the A Train," which were the band's theme song, was written by band member Billy Strayhorn.

_____ **43.** When Ellington died in 1974, the news were received sorrowfully by jazz fans around the world.

_____ **44.** Three decades has passed since people had the opportunity to hear Ellington's piano artistry in person.

_____ **45.** How I would like to be one of they!

_____ **46.** In recent years swing music, including many of Ellington's songs, have gained renewed popularity.

_____ **47.** Surely he would be pleased that many of the songs he wrote is still in great demand.

_____ **48.** In fact, his songs are often requested by the crowd that come to our school's weekly jazz band concerts.

_____ **49.** The band are always happy to comply with those requests.

_____ **50.** As a result, many a student have come to appreciate what a maestro Ellington was.

Using Pronouns Correctly: Case Forms of Pronouns

A. SELECTING CORRECT FORMS OF PRONOUNS Underline the correct form of the pronoun in parentheses in each of the following sentences.

Example 1. Mrs. Tanaka gave Ruth and (*I*, *me*) a ride home from the library.

1. We don't play our music nearly as loudly as the neighbors play (*their*, *theirs*).

2. The Gonzalez twins treated (*theirselves*, *themselves*) to lunch at that new French cafe that just opened near their apartment building.

3. We appreciate (*you*, *your*) having us over for dinner last night.

4. What makes you think that the one who started the rumor was (*he*, *him*)?

5. You are the only one in this class (*who*, *whom*) I am inviting to my party.

6. My advice to you is not to worry about what (*they*, *them*) think.

7. Please keep (*me*, *my*) entering the contest a secret for now.

8. The McKays are the neighbors (*who*, *whom*) I would turn to in an emergency.

9. No one else I've ever known has been a better friend to me than (*she*, *her*).

10. Don't forget to send (*we*, *us*) less adventurous homebodies postcards while you're on your trip to India.

11. Mr. Washington said he wants to speak with you and (*I*, *me*) about our work schedules for next month's holiday vacation.

12. My stepdad and (*I*, *me*) spent Saturday morning cleaning out our garage.

13. At our house, the telephone is answered by (*whoever*, *whomever*) is closest to it.

14. While we were waiting at the bus stop, Leo drew Rachel and (*I*, *me*) a map of the new outlet mall.

15. Joe and I appreciate (*you*, *your*) helping us carry those boxes inside.

16. (*Who*, *Whom*) are you planning to ask to the prom?

17. After swimming and snorkeling for a while, (*we*, *us*) vacationers organized a game of beach volleyball.

18. Although the other team had the home-field advantage, we scored more points than (*they*, *them*) and won the trophy.

19. Have you seen Katie and (*she*, *her*) this morning?

20. Last weekend, Yoko and (*I*, *myself*) went skiing for the first time.

B. PROOFREADING SENTENCES FOR CORRECT PRONOUN FORMS   Most of the following sentences contain an error in pronoun usage. Draw a line through each incorrect pronoun, and write the correct form above it. If an item is already correct, write *C* on the line provided.

                                          I

Example _____ **1.** I think you and ~~me~~ can get a ride home with Carla.

_____ **21.** Don't you agree that us juniors should be allowed to go off campus for lunch?

_____ **22.** Several people have asked me whom I predict will win the election.

_____ **23.** Once again the squirrels have gorged theirselves on the birdseed in the feeder.

_____ **24.** The co-captains, June and her, received the biggest round of applause.

_____ **25.** Uncle Pablo and Aunt Ines usually send my brother Felix and I gift certificates for our birthdays.

_____ **26.** My mom said your mom and yourself are welcome to come over to see my new baby brother anytime.

_____ **27.** Are you sure it was Len who you saw talking to Sue Ellen in the cafeteria?

_____ **28.** Most members of the debate team attributed the victory at the state competition to their having practiced so vigorously beforehand.

_____ **29.** I asked Dwayne to go kayaking with you and I on Saturday, but he said that he has to work.

_____ **30.** Some of my friends speak French far more fluently than me.

_____ **31.** Tell Martha and them to meet us at the box office at 7:30 Wednesday night.

_____ **32.** Either Kwan or me will be happy to give you and them a ride home.

_____ **33.** No one else worked as hard on the project as he.

_____ **34.** Coach Crawford said that he wants to meet with we linebackers before practice this afternoon.

_____ **35.** The club honored two members, Dora and she, for their outstanding service.

_____ **36.** I still can't get over you trying to call me at exactly the same time I was trying to call you yesterday.

_____ **37.** It's after six; shouldn't Bao and her be here by now?

_____ **38.** The people I waved to at the restaurant turned out not to be them.

_____ **39.** I'm not sure whether this is my set of keys or yours.

_____ **40.** Please tell whomever calls that I'll be home by ten o'clock.

C. PROOFREADING SENTENCES FOR CORRECT PRONOUN FORMS Most of the following sentences contain errors in pronoun usage. Draw a line through each incorrect pronoun form, and write the correct form above it. If a sentence is already correct, write *C* on the line provided.

Example _____ **1.** The people ~~whom~~ *who* are our houseguests this week are the Parkers.

_____ **41.** It was them who lived next door to us in Oklahoma City.

_____ **42.** Their youngest daughter, Rosa, and myself were close friends.

_____ **43.** In fact, we used to spend so much time together that our parents called we girls the
two musketeers.

_____ **44.** Mr. Parker grew up in Seattle, and he was the main one whom wanted to relocate
there when he retired from the Air Force last year.

_____ **45.** As it turned out, the move proved to be a good one for all of them.

_____ **46.** The whole family has taken up skiing, and Mr. Parker has even gotten hisself qualified
as a member of a ski patrol.

_____ **47.** He has been telling us exciting stories about them rescuing hapless skiers.

_____ **48.** I have never heard anyone who is a better storyteller than him.

_____ **49.** The Parkers have invited my parents and I to visit them in Seattle next December, and
we can't wait.

_____ **50.** Neither them nor I have ever tried skiing.

Clear Reference: Pronouns and Antecedents

A. CORRECTING FAULTY PRONOUN REFERENCES Each of the following items contains an ambiguous, general, weak, or indefinite reference. On the line provided, rewrite each item to correct the faulty pronoun reference. If an item is already correct, write *C* on the line.

Example 1. In the documentary, they explore the lives of migrant workers.

The documentary explores the lives of migrant workers.

1. My great-aunt swims two miles a day, and it keeps her fit and trim.

2. Devin is always so thoughtful. One is that he always remembers his friends' birthdays.

3. Melina told Emily that Ms. Cardenas wanted to see her.

4. Whenever I hear a recording by that band, I wish I were one of them.

5. At Olympic National Park in Washington state, they have hundreds of miles of trails.

6. Each chapter of the novel ends with a cliffhanger. That makes the book hard to put down.

7. My grandfather saw Neil Armstrong on television when he walked on the moon.

8. When finals are over, it will be a great relief to all of us.

9. We visited the humane society and came home with two adorable ones.

10. I found Web sites that offer virtual tours of colleges. This helped me narrow my choices.

11. Miguel and I spent an hour browsing at the bookstore but did not buy any.

12. Tom takes piano lessons from Mr. Howard, and he thinks that he is doing very well.

13. The fleeing wild horses, smelling more smoke, increased it to a gallop.

_____

14. When the car's left rear fender hit the mailbox, it crumpled.

_____

15. In this article it describes what a remarkable career soprano Leontyne Price has had.

_____

16. My parents liked the neighborhood but couldn't find one there that suited our needs.

_____

17. Mr. Hawk, our guest speaker, explained what someone has to do to become a programmer.

_____

18. Later, he took questions from the audience. This helped clarify some of his statements.

_____

19. In Williamsburg, Virginia, you can see how people lived during colonial times.

_____

20. When Carlotta introduced Maxine to us, we asked her where she was from.

_____

B. CORRECTING FAULTY PRONOUN REFERENCES Most of the following items contain pronouns without clear antecedents. On the line provided, revise each item to correct any unclear pronoun references. If an item is already correct, write *C* on the line.

Example 1. You and I have been friends for more than ten years, which is amazing.

That you and I have been friends for more than ten years is amazing.

21. In N. Scott Momaday's *The Way to Rainy Mountain*, it retells a number of Kiowa folk tales.

_____

22. Someone turned in my missing wallet, which was such a relief.

_____

23. Frederico gave Alan a ride home, and he told him about his plans for the weekend.

_____

24. Mrs. Tranh told me about growing up in Vietnam, and this gave me the idea for my topic.

_____

25. In the newspaper it reported that the mayor will not seek reelection.

26. Some of my friends are already taking junior college courses, which is a wise move.

27. The club members discussed several topics. One of these was who would be treasurer.

28. When my dad's car wouldn't start, that made me late for school.

29. Roland is a talented portraitist who can bring them to life on canvas.

30. One reason the movie was fun to watch was that they seemed to be having fun themselves.

31. That the first Americans likely came to North America from Asia is widely accepted by historians.

32. Ruth met Alice at the shoe store, where she was shopping for a pair of sandals.

33. I've always been interested in archaeology, but I do not plan to be one.

34. The speaker, seeing the large crowd, became so rattled that it made him forget his speech.

35. We had planned to serve our guests appetizers in the living room, but the cat ate them.

36. Along with the egg rolls, we ordered lemon chicken and fried rice. It was delicious.

37. He is a well-organized student, planning it carefully.

38. At my high school they have a faculty meeting at least once a week.

39. Mom and Dad will be gone this weekend. That leaves me in charge of my brothers.

40. In 1999 you could hardly avoid hearing about the so-called millennium bug.

Using Verbs Correctly: Principal Parts, Tense, Voice, Mood

A. USING IRREGULAR VERBS CORRECTLY Underline the correct verb form in parentheses in each of the following sentences.

Example 1. By this time tomorrow, I (*had run, will have run*) my first marathon.

1. Not until I had (*drove, driven*) halfway home did I remember my promise to give Rose a ride.

2. My uncle Harvey has (*sang, sung*) at many of his friends' weddings.

3. Did you happen to notice where I (*lay, laid*) my keys?

4. Interest rates have (*risen, rose*) twice so far this year.

5. After we have (*swam, swum*) for a while, we will have our picnic.

6. During the early twentieth century, many African Americans (*buyed, bought*) cosmetics manu-

factured by Sarah Breedlove Walker, better known as Madame C. J. Walker.

7. If he (*was, were*) wise, he would find a more reliable Internet service provider.

8. Some of these items have (*laid, lain*) in the lost-and-found box for months.

9. If you had (*ran, run*) for class president, I would have voted for you.

10. Our guest speaker today has (*spoke, spoken*) to high school students throughout the nation.

11. As soon as Coach Mack (*drawed, drew*) us a diagram of the play, we knew what to do.

12. Every morning Luna writes a short journal entry about what she (*did, done*) the day before.

13. Your clean laundry has been (*sitting, setting*) in a basket in the laundry room since Saturday.

14. Grandma will be surprised to see how much my little sister has (*grew, grown*).

15. If you haven't (*ate, eaten*) yet, you are welcome to stay for supper.

B. PROOFREADING SENTENCES FOR VERB USAGE For each of the following sentences, draw a line through each incorrect verb form or verbal, and then write the correct form above it.

Example 1. Ladies and Gentlemen, please ~~raise~~ *rise* for our national anthem.

16. If you would have read the book, you would understand why the critics panned the movie.

17. I had planned to have begun my research paper much sooner.

18. Naomi wishes that she had saw last week's performance by the Ballet Folklorico of Mexico.

19. Please try to be quiet; I just lay the baby down for his nap.

20. You should have went with us to the amusement park last Saturday; we had fun.

21. The temperature has been raising steadily since this morning's low.

22. My uncle said that if he was mayor, he would lower property taxes.

23. When you leave for school this morning, remember to have taken out the garbage.

24. All semester, I have rose early to get in an extra hour of studying.

25. For many years Yo-Yo Ma's virtuoso cello playing has brung great joy to his listeners.

26. By this time next year, we will become seniors at last.

27. The island of Manhattan lays between the East River and the Hudson River.

28. Listening to the car radio on the way home from school yesterday, I had heard an interview with Sandra Cisneros.

29. Our neighbors' recycling bin has been setting at the curb all week.

30. Megan tries on several outfits before finding one that she liked well enough to buy.

31. The defendant claims to be out of the country at the time of the crime.

32. If I had your address, I would have sent you a postcard from Puerto Rico.

33. By the time we had arrived at the restaurant, the servers had closed the breakfast buffet.

34. Mr. Gonzalez suggested that I wrote about growing up on military bases all over the country.

35. Replacing the flat tire with the spare, we resumed our journey.

C. REVISING SENTENCES IN THE PASSIVE VOICE On the line provided, revise each of the following sentences by changing the passive voice to active voice.

Example 1. We were shown several houses by the real estate agent.

The real estate agent showed us several houses.

36. It was announced by the White House press secretary that the President has the flu.

_____

37. The birdhouse that Lonnie built has been moved into by bluebirds.

_____

38. The e-mail message that you sent us was received by both Lee and me.

_____

39. You and Michelle were seen at the mall by us yesterday.

_____

40. The enchiladas that were prepared by Aunt Flora were enjoyed by the entire family.

_____

41. We were advised by Mr. Rawlings to get a good night's sleep before the test.

_____

42. Each of the soldiers will be awarded a medal by the President.

_____

43. The keynote speech at the state convention was delivered by Nora McPherson.

_____

44. By whom were you given that lovely silver and turquoise Navajo bracelet?

_____

45. That the accident had been caused by a speeding driver was reported by the newspaper.

_____

D. IDENTIFYING THE MOOD OF VERBS Identify the mood of the italicized verb or verb phrase in each of the following sentences. On the line provided, write *IND* for *indicative*, *IMP* for *imperative*, or *SUB* for *subjunctive*.

Example _SUB_ **1.** I suggest that Marla *draft* the resolution.

_____ **46.** Dexter, please *mail* these letters for me.

_____ **47.** When I heard the news, I felt as if I *were* on top of the world.

_____ **48.** *Do* you *know* the capital of California?

_____ **49.** Stacey *wishes* that she were less quick-tempered.

_____ **50.** Doctor Okada recommended that Grandpa *get* a flu shot.

Using Modifiers Correctly: Forms and Uses of Adjectives and Adverbs; Comparison

A. USING MODIFIERS CORRECTLY Underline the correct modifier in parentheses in each of the following sentences.

Example 1. You might have more energy if you exercised more (*regular, regularly*).

1. We saw several (*real, really*) spectacular sunsets when we were in Key West, Florida.

2. Shouting (*gleeful, gleefully*), the first-graders raced for the playground swings.

3. The rusted muffler makes our car noisier than (*any, any other*) car on our block.

4. If you listen (*close, closely*), you may be able to hear a hummingbird's wings beating.

5. We should arrive there (*certain, certainly*) by late afternoon.

6. Of all the dishes on the Chinese lunch buffet, I liked the crab Rangoon (*better, best*).

7. Before you use a new cleaning product, always read the label (*close, closely*).

8. Smoky is the (*more gentle, most gentle*) one of our four stallions at my aunt and uncle's stables.

9. According to the weather report for this weekend, it should be (*less, least*) windy on Sunday.

10. How (*good, well*) do you think you did on the test?

11. I went back and revised my answer to make it (*correct, more correct*).

12. As soon as I started down the slope, I realized how (*bad, badly*) I had misjudged.

13. Training my new puppy has helped me become much (*patienter, more patient*).

14. With whose writing are you (*more familiar, most familiar*), Maxine Hong Kingston's or Amy Tan's?

15. This computer seems to be working more (*slow, slowly*) than usual.

B. REVISING SENTENCES TO CORRECT MODIFIER ERRORS Most of the following sentences contain an awkward, informal, or incorrect use of a modifier. Draw a line through each error, and above it write the correction. If a sentence is already correct, write *C* on the line provided.

          qualified as
Example _____ **1.** You are as ~~qualified,~~ if not more qualified than, the other applicants are.

_____ **16.** I narrowed down the choice to two sandwiches and finally picked the least expensive one.

_____ **17.** With a final score of 286, the game was the most perfect one I have ever bowled.

_____ **18.** My knee hurt so bad after I fell that I decided to have it X-rayed.

_____ **19.** Which of the colleges in the New York area has the more highly regarded film school?

_____ **20.** Sounding nostalgic, Grandpa described his early childhood in Cuba.

_____ **21.** I can't meet you any more earlier than 7:30 on Saturday morning.

_____ **22.** The bibliography for my research paper is as long, if not longer than, the teacher requires.

_____ **23.** Before you cut any of the boards for the bookcase, be sure that you measure and mark each one precise.

_____ **24.** The Indian music scale has twenty-two steps to an octave and is therefore more complex than Western music, which has only twelve steps.

_____ **25.** People interested in increasing their vocabulary are often advised to read wide and often.

_____ **26.** At the Italian festival, we especially enjoyed watching a real fast dance known as the tarantella.

_____ **27.** Even when his schedule becomes hectic, Fred somehow remains calmly and plows through the heavy workload.

_____ **28.** Those garlic breadsticks you're baking smell wonderfully, Uncle Enrique.

_____ **29.** I think I would rather have my chop suey with rice than with noodles.

_____ **30.** Why does time always seem to pass so quick when you're having fun?

C. CORRECTING MODIFIER ERRORS Most of the following sentences contain at least one error in the use of modifiers. Draw a line through each error, and then write the correct form above the error. If a sentence is already correct, write *C* on the line provided.

Example _____ **1.** My new electronic organizer helps me plan my time ~~real good~~. *really well*

_____ **31.** Be sure you clamp the wood tight in the vise before you begin sanding.

_____ **32.** Principal Lewis took our concerns about the safety of the old bleachers very serious.

_____ **33.** Which of the rides at the state fair did you find more exciting?

_____ **34.** After Molly gave her report on the First Amendment, Mr. Daniels asked whether any of the students had questions.

_____ **35.** Cats are notorious for acting aloof toward their human companions from time to time.

_____ **36.** Which of the twins is the most outgoing, Anita or Angela?

_____ **37.** Mom said that the 6:30 A.M. shuttle was the most earliest flight she could get.

_____ **38.** To me, the smell of fresh cut grass is one of summer's pleasantest sensations.

_____ **39.** Whenever I retire a pair of running shoes, I notice that the left one is least worn-out.

_____ **40.** I don't spend as much time with Keith as Ben.

D. CORRECTING ERRORS IN THE USE OF MODIFIERS Draw a line through each error in the use of modifiers in the following sentences. Then, above the error, write the correct form of the modifier. If a sentence is already correct, write *C* on the line provided.

Example _____ **1.** Kenesha's classmates seemed ~~real~~ *really* interested in her report about Senegal.

_____ **41.** Dakar, located at Africa's most western point, is not only Senegal's capital but also the more strategically located of all of Senegal's coastal cities.

_____ **42.** The class listened intent while Kenesha explained how Senegal, a small but historically powerful country, achieved its independence from France in 1960.

_____ **43.** The first president, Léopold Senghor, slowly revised the new country's institutions to serve the needs of its population better.

_____ **44.** The Senegalese, who rely more on peanuts than on any crop for their income from agricultural exports, have experienced a decline in their economy since independence.

_____ **45.** Of Senegal's five geographical regions, the southwestern Casamance with its ample rainfall is better suited for growing rice.

_____ **46.** While Senegal is home to at least seven major ethnic groups, relations between these groups have on the whole remained peacefully.

_____ **47.** To add flavor and variety to their primarily grain-based diet, many Senegalese cooks season their sauces good.

_____ **48.** The most tastiest and most unusual Senegalese drink is *niamban*—a mixture of tamarind juice, smoked fish, salt, and cayenne.

_____ **49.** As in most of Africa, soccer is the popularest sport in Senegal.

_____ **50.** Of these two authors—Aminata Sow Fall and Ousmane Sembene—who has done the best job of presenting Senegal to the rest of the world?

Placement of Modifiers: Misplaced and Dangling Modifiers

A. REVISING SENTENCES BY CORRECTING MISPLACED MODIFIERS The following sentences contain misplaced modifiers. On the line provided, revise each sentence so that its meaning is clear and correct.

Example 1. Grateful, the firefighters were profusely thanked by the homeowners.

The grateful homeowners profusely thanked the firefighters.

1. Ernie told me about his piano recital on the bus this morning.

_____

2. The candidates pledged to avoid negative advertising in their press conference.

_____

3. Rene said after Latin class she will meet us in the library.

_____

4. I found a copy of Willa Cather's *My Ántonia* browsing in a bookstore.

_____

5. Max rescued a turtle trying to cross the highway on the way to the dry cleaners.

_____

6. I finally looked for the jeans I wanted to wear in the clothes dryer.

_____

7. Hungry and clever, even a lock on the garbage can did not thwart the raccoon.

_____

8. We heard a lion roar while eating lunch at the zoo's cafeteria.

_____

9. The bandleader complained at rehearsal the horn section sounded off-key.

_____

10. We were surprised to see how much damage the tornado did on the evening news.

_____

11. My sister and I have only run in one 10K race this year.

_____

12. Jaime told us on Saturday he found a good used drill at the flea market.

_____

13. I have almost picked all the photographs for my project on the wheat harvest.

_____

14. Mom reminded Joey before he left for school to feed the cat.

_____

15. Naomi and I smelled the aroma of baked apples walking into the kitchen.

_____

16. The professor gave a lecture about tidal waves in the auditorium.

_____

17. The manager said yesterday too many employees arrived late.

_____

18. The principal announced that morning we will have a fire drill.

_____

19. Ralph Waldo Emerson asserted that people should trust their intuition in his book *Nature*.

_____

20. My parents only let me stay out until 10:30 on school nights.

_____

B. **REVISING SENTENCES BY CORRECTING DANGLING MODIFIERS**   Most of the following sentences contain dangling modifiers. On the line provided, revise each faulty sentence so that its meaning is clear and correct. If a sentence is already correct, write *C* on the line.

Example 1. To enter the essay contest, manuscripts must be submitted by May 1.

   To enter the essay contest, writers must submit manuscripts by May 1.

21. Hearing the can opener, the cat's meows grew louder.

_____

22. Exhausted but happy, the finish line lay only a few yards ahead of the runners.

_____

23. While helping my stepdad wash his car, my friend Sal dropped by to visit.

_____

24. Passing a wand over the top hat, a floppy-eared white rabbit appeared.

_____

25. After heating the wok, the scallions, garlic, and snow peas were quickly stir-fried.

_____

26. To vote in next month's primary election, today is the last day to register.

_____

27. Answering the telephone, the caller's voice wasn't recognized at first.

_____

28. When driving a long distance, rest breaks should be taken at regular intervals.

_____

29. Getting off the bus, my notebook fell in a puddle.

_____

30. To be an effective speaker, eye contact with the audience should be maintained.

_____

31. Forced to leave their homelands, the Cherokee reestablished themselves in Oklahoma.

_____

32. To succeed in almost any endeavor, self-discipline and perseverance are needed.

_____

33. Before enlisting in the Air Force, Florida had been Laura's home all her life.

_____

34. Alarmed by the rise in shoplifting, security cameras were installed in the store.

_____

35. To become a geologist, at least a bachelor's degree in geology is necessary.

_____

36. Having landed on the moon, the lunar surface was explored.

_____

37. While leaving the house, my backpack strap got hooked on the doorknob.

_____

38. Looking at the TV schedule, a documentary about the Dalai Lama is on later this evening.

_____

39. Talking quite loudly, we couldn't help but overhear the man's phone conversation.

_____

40. Clear and still, we watched the fish swimming around the reef under our boat.

_____

A Glossary of Usage: Common Usage Problems

A. IDENTIFYING CORRECT USAGE For each of the following sentences, underline the word or word group in parentheses that is correct according to the rules of standard, formal English.

Example 1. The city commission has voted to make Grand Avenue (*a, an*) one-way street.

1. The low-fat version of the recipe has half the (*amount, number*) of calories of the original.

2. This article on the origins of the Internet is (*kind of, somewhat*) interesting.

3. My supervisor has scheduled me to work (*fewer, less*) hours this week than last week.

4. Grandma said that she would (*borrow, lend*) me her pearl earrings for the prom.

5. Television coverage of the famine (*affected, effected*) many viewers deeply.

6. Vernon is working hard to become an Eagle Scout (*as, like*) his older brother did.

7. I'm sorry, but the man who gave us the free tickets (*doesn't, don't*) have any more of them to give away.

8. Historian Ernesto Galarza's parents (*emigrated, immigrated*) to the United States when Ernesto was six years old.

9. Biblical (*allusions, illusions*) are quite common in contemporary literature.

10. (*Being as, Since*) you have finished your research report, would you please give me some feedback on mine?

11. The superintendent of schools (*implied, inferred*) that she planned to run for reelection.

12. (*Among, Between*) them, the Begay twins have completed two hundred hours of volunteer service at the hospital this year.

13. Yes, it was Jan Ernst Matzeliger who (*discovered, invented*) the shoe-lasting machine.

14. If we're going to be late, we (*had ought, ought*) to let our parents know.

15. As Indira explained, (*that, those*) kinds of spices are often used in Indian cooking.

16. My chemistry teacher, (*which, who*) is Mr. Hisako, has been named Teacher of the Year.

17. Please (*accept, except*) my sincere congratulations on your promotion.

18. Both my mother and Aunt Thelma are (*alumnae, alumni*) of Howard University.

19. During the weekend Dad and I came down with some (*kind of, kind of a*) virus.

20. The scout master told the campers that they would have to put up their tents by (*theirselves, themselves*).

21. I heard on the radio (*that, where*) the Oscar® nominations will be announced tomorrow.

22. How many people in your driver education class have (*all ready, already*) gotten a license?

23. After we had finished the yardwork, we jumped (*in, into*) the pool to cool off.

24. Meteorologists are warning that the hurricane may intensify (*some, somewhat*) during the next few days.

25. Who else did you invite to go camping (*beside, besides*) Tomás and me?

B. CORRECTING ERRORS IN USAGE The following sentences contain gender-specific terms and errors in the use of standard, formal English. Draw a line through each such term or error, and write the correct usage above it.

Example 1. Our biology teacher explained the differences ~~among~~ a shark, a ray, and a chimaera.
between

26. The reason we were late for the wedding was because we missed our connecting flight.

27. Mom told my sister, "Don't forget to bring this signed report card back to school tomorrow morning."

28. My two cousins have wanted to be firemen since they were six years old.

29. The fog was so thick that we couldn't hardly see the road.

30. Saffron is one type spice that is widely used in Indian cooking.

31. I must of left my study notes at Ronnie's house last night.

32. Pilar is hoping to be excepted by her father's alma mater, Dartmouth College.

33. Renowned sculptor Isamu Noguchi he studied medicine before pursuing a career in the arts.

34. Vinnie accidentally cut hisself when he was chopping onions.

35. As soon as the rain looks like it is tapering off, the game will be resumed.

36. My grandfather use to be a choreographer for a dance troupe in Hartford.

37. The shore did not look a long ways off but took a long time to reach in that strong current.

38. Lily did much better on the test then she had expected to.

39. The salesmen at that store seem more helpful than the ones at the store at the other mall.

40. Aboard the space shuttle *Endeavour* in 1992, former astronaut Mae Jemison studied the affects of weightlessness on bone tissue.

41. Morrie's batting average has improved some since he started lifting weights.

42. An oxymoron is where a person combines opposite ideas in a single figure of speech.

43. Driving along a highway on a hot day, you may see the allusion of water on the road ahead.

44. We don't have plans to go nowhere this summer.

45. Hopefully, I will be able to find all the reference material I need at the public library.

46. According to this here article, the only thing that can cut a diamond is another diamond.

47. We asked the desk clerk at the hotel where we stayed in Phoenix where the Pueblo Grande Museum was at.

48. Through the Human Genome Project, scientists hoped to invent the chemical instructions that determine inherited characteristics.

49. We are planning to plant less flowers and more vegetables in the garden this year.

50. We have looked everywheres except up in the attic for the old photograph album.

Capitalization: Rules of Standard Usage

A. CAPITALIZING WORDS AND NAMES CORRECTLY Most of the following numbered items contain errors in capitalization. If an item contains an error, rewrite the item on the line provided. If an item is already correct, write *C*.

Example 1. uncle fred, my father's brother in san diego *Uncle Fred, my father's brother in*
                                                              San Diego

1. a small town in the south _____

2. the democratic primary _____

3. a herculean effort _____

4. dear mrs. huang: _____

5. the northeast corner of state street and forty-second avenue _____

_____

6. governor-elect platero _____

7. albany, the capital of new york _____

8. the space shuttle *endeavour* _____

9. my uncle ernesto _____

10. in history class today _____

11. neptune, the roman god of the sea _____

12. air force medal of honor _____

13. a movie studio in culver city _____

14. Robert frost's "the death of the hired man" _____

15. a mild winter _____

16. the big dipper _____

17. nabisco™ crackers _____

18. the coast of jordan along the dead sea _____

19. the last sunday in april _____

20. the planet saturn as seen from earth _____

21. the british ambassador _____

22. university of cincinnati _____

23. first chapter of genesis in the holy bible _____

_____

24. she replied, "yes, i have seen *gone with the wind*." _____

_____

25. american federation of state, county, and municipal employees _____

_____

B. CORRECTING ERRORS IN CAPITALIZATION   Each of the following sentences contains at least one error in capitalization. Correct the errors either by changing capital letters to lowercase letters or by changing lowercase letters to capital letters.

Example 1. Betelgeuse is a bright ~~S~~tar in the ~~C~~onstellation of ~~o~~rion.
(corrections above: s, c, O)

26. On Memorial day we visited the Wheelwright museum of the American Indian in santa fe, new Mexico.

27. According to Roman Mythology, Juno was married to Jupiter, King of the Gods.

28. In his epic Poem the *aeneid*, Virgil portrays Juno as an adversary of the trojan hero Aeneas.

29. My Uncle Vernon bought his 1966 Mustang convertible at Eubie's used cars in Park rapids.

30. Tradition ascribes the authorship of the pentateuch, the first five Books of the bible, to the israelite leader Moses.

31. Experimental physicist Chien-Shiung Wu, who earned her Ph.d. from the university of California, demonstrated that the law of the conservation of parity was inaccurate.

32. On channel 11 last night, we watched a documentary about Nellie Bly, who in 1889 set out to circumnavigate the Globe as an investigative reporter for the *New York world*.

33. Completing the trip in 72 days, 6 hours, and 11 minutes, Bly outpaced the record set by Phileas Fogg, the hero of Jules Verne's 1873 novel *Around The World in Eighty Days*.

34. Our guest speaker today is Ex-senator Georgia A. Turner, who will outline the president's plans for negotiating a peace settlement in the middle east.

35. Our Dentist, dr. Alex Pappas, is retiring next month; his Son Christopher will be taking over his father's practice.

36. Several of us Juniors are planning a farewell party for our chemistry II teacher, Mrs. Alvarado.

37. While skiing at the lone Pine Resort in the Rocky mountains last December, Jeremy fell and broke his collarbone.

38. My friend Luisa, who wants to be a Photographer, has been saving her allowance to buy a Nikon™ Camera.

39. Our dog pepper is part irish setter and part Dalmatian.

40. Located in Eastern Iowa, the Company is renowned for the high quality of its products.

41. From 1989 to 1993, Army general Colin Powell served as Chairman of the Joint Chiefs of Staff.

42. This recipe calls for belgian endive, which i don't think Greg's groceries carries.

43. What a great time we had at the museum of Science and Industry in Chicago!

44. Have you read Edgar Allan Poe's classic Short Story "The Murders in The Rue Morgue"?

45. I read recently that the story is generally considered the first Modern detective story.

C. USING ABBREVIATIONS IN FORMAL WRITING Rewrite the following sentences, correcting errors in the use and capitalization of abbreviations.

Example 1. Ms Sullivan introduced us to Capt Perez from El Paso, Tx.

Ms. Sullivan introduced us to Captain Perez from El Paso, Texas.

46. In the metric system, a meter is approximately 39.37 in, or a little more than a yd.

_____

47. Does the fbi have an office in the capital of La, Baton Rouge?

_____

48. Our first President, Geo. Washington, presided over a nation of only about four million people.

_____

49. The address on the box read, "To prof. Cook, 512 N Ridge Rd, Lutz, Fla 33549."

_____

50. The flight arrives at 3:15 P.M.; the cab ride to the hotel takes 45 min or so.

_____

Punctuation: End Marks and Commas

A. USING PERIODS, QUESTION MARKS, EXCLAMATION POINTS, AND COMMAS CORRECTLY The following sentences lack periods, question marks, exclamation points, and commas. Insert the correct punctuation in each sentence.

Example 1. This hot, humid weather is hard on our oldest dog, Sam.

1. The telephone call was for Hector and Maria took the message

2. What a terrific movie that was

3. My favorite aunt Lila has invited me to visit her next summer in Portland Maine

4. The name of the world's largest country, China, comes from the Qin dynasty, which lasted only from 221 BC to 206 BC.

5. As I was returning my library books I realized that I had left one of them at home

6. Ernie wanted to go to the mall with us after school but he had to work

7. All students auditioning for the play should report to the auditorium no later than 4:00 P M today

8. Shall we go swimming or bowling or hiking on Saturday

9. Well I certainly hope you know what you're doing

10. Marv yelled "Wow This band is terrific"

11. I'll support your candidacy for I think you'd make a great class president

12. My understanding Amy is that the assignment is due Friday not Monday

13. In any case the deadline is approaching rapidly

14. Drenched the dog shook itself vigorously spraying muddy water all over the clean kitchen floor and the cabinets

15. Are you familiar with the expression "A stitch in time saves nine"

16. At the end of the interview be sure to thank your subject for his or her time

17. Patricia R Harris who received her law degree from George Washington University in Washington D C was the first African American woman to serve in the U S Cabinet

18. Juan's best subjects this year are English Latin and geometry

19. The novel that I am reading is a fast-paced gripping narrative set in the Bronx

20. Mr Olathe our scout leader asked us what our plans are for the summer

21. "By the way have you been on the new hike-and-bike trail the one along the river" Sally asked

22. Please let me know when you have finished using the copier Mel

23. Flo's new address is 1549 N Glendale Ave Riverview MI 48192

24. Are you sure the guest speaker at this afternoon's seminar is the Arthur Henderson M D who wrote the recent bestselling diet book

25. Mom usually has to remind my brother "Get your booster seat sit up straight and fasten your seat belt"

B. PROOFREADING SENTENCES FOR THE CORRECT USE OF END MARKS AND COMMAS Most of the following sentences contain at least one error in the use of end marks or commas. Correct each error by adding or deleting an end mark or comma. If a sentence is already correct, write *C* on the line provided.

Example 1. You may be right, Wanda, but your argument, I think, is weak.

26. We hiked to the lake, and spent the afternoon swimming.

27. Naturally revising your writing requires both time and patience.

28. Run for your life Justin

29. Don't forget to ask the salesperson what the store's return policy is?

30. Today's special is meatloaf, mashed potatoes, and gravy and steamed green beans.

31. The distance, as far as I can tell, from the map is about thirty miles.

32. Rosa is interested in studying medicine yet she is also drawn to meteorology.

33. For his performance as a drill sergeant in a 1982 film, Louis Gossett Jr won the Academy Award® for Best Supporting Actor.

34. For dessert we had wedges of cold refreshing seedless watermelon.

35. Startled Felicia explained that she had been deep in thought, when I tapped her on the shoulder.

36. Please help me carry in the groceries, that are in the car

37. Did they really think that New Mexico is a foreign country not a state

38. From 1975 to 1977 acclaimed, Mexican author Carlos Fuentes served as his country's ambassador to France.

39. How you speak, and how you carry yourself are important factors in the impression you make on other people

40. Do you know who wrote the words to "The Star-Spangled Banner?"

41. Over the weekend the woman who lives across the hall from us Mrs Sato, taught me how to make shrimp tempura.

42. No softball practice won't begin until four this afternoon will it Brittany

43. Frances Ellen Watkins Harper who lived from 1825 to 1911 is considered by many as the foremost African American poet of her era

44. Harper was also a popular lecturer speaking passionately against slavery and for women's suffrage.

45. Running for the bus I tripped, and, broke my left wrist.

46. After all, your hard work you deserve to win the Volunteer of the Year Award.

47. With the signing of the Treaty of Guadalupe Hidalgo by Mexico and the United States on February 2, 1848 the Mexican War, which had begun in 1846 officially ended.

48. Oh, where in the world did you get that finely, carved antique brass sword?

49. As soon as I have finished washing these dishes I will take you for a long walk Spot.

50. My best friend Ralph is originally from Kingston the capital of Jamaica

Punctuation: Other Marks of Punctuation

A. USING SEMICOLONS AND COLONS CORRECTLY   Correct the punctuation in the following sentences by adding semicolons and colons where they are needed and by changing other punctuation and capitalization as needed.

Example **1.** The following items were among those rationed in the United States during World War II ⸴ coffee, cars, sugar, and tires.

1. Jolene works twenty hours a week as a result, she has saved several hundred dollars for college.

2. The letter from the sweepstakes company began "Dear Finalist" it went on to tell me that I might already have won $10,000,000.

3. In Washington, D.C., we visited three museums in a single day the National Portrait Gallery, the Freer Gallery of Art, and the National Museum of Natural History.

4. Pastor Elrod's sermon today was based on Matthew 5 3, which is the opening verse of the Sermon on the Mount.

5. You may not recognize Esther Pauline Friedman Lederer's name you have probably read, however, the column she writes under her pen name, Ann Landers.

6. During the week I set my alarm clock for 6 15 A.M., but on the weekends I don't set it at all.

7. The Fourth of July parade included floats, which all had a patriotic theme, marching bands, clowns, jugglers, and other circus performers, and antique cars, trucks, and other vehicles.

8. Cesar Chavez understood the plight of Mexican American farmworkers He had been one himself.

9. At the library I found a fascinating book called *Coming to America Immigrants from Eastern Europe*, by Shirley Blumenthal.

10. When Jimmy Carter was inaugurated as the governor of Georgia in January of 1971, he spoke these ringing words "No poor, rural, weak, or black person should ever have to bear the additional burden of being deprived of the opportunity of an education, a job, or simple justice."

B. USING UNDERLINING (ITALICS) AND QUOTATION MARKS CORRECTLY   Add underlining (italics) and quotation marks where they are needed in each of the following sentences. Change other punctuation and capitalization if necessary. If a sentence is already correct, write *C* on the line provided.

Example _____ **1.** "In bowling, rolling three strikes in a row is known as a turkey," said Al.

_____ **11.** Your essay on charter schools, said Rowena, Was certainly thought-provoking.

_____ **12.** Read the chapter titled Analysis of a Novel tonight, and be prepared to discuss it in class tomorrow, said Mr. Higgins.

_____ **13.** Succeeding Against the Odds is a fascinating autobiography by John H. Johnson, publisher of Ebony and Jet, among other magazines.

_____ **14.** Mom remarked, "I can never remember whether the word 'unnecessary' has one n or two.

_____ **15.** Scientists have spent years working to re-establish the ecological balance in Alaska's Prince William Sound, after the oil tanker Exxon Valdez spilled millions of gallons of crude oil in 1989.

_____ **16.** Several of my friends have told me that I use the expression you know too much.

_____ **17.** Semper Fidelis, the motto of the United States Marine Corps since 1880, is Latin for Always Faithful.

_____ **18.** Rachel said that she plans to study engineering at Stanford University.

_____ **19.** "Turn that radio down! shouted the apartment manager.

_____ **20.** In his book The Way of All Flesh, Samuel Butler writes, "the advantage of doing one's praising for oneself is that one can lay it on so thick and exactly in the right places.

C. USING APOSTROPHES, HYPHENS, DASHES, BRACKETS, AND PARENTHESES CORRECTLY   Correct each error in the use of apostrophes, hyphens, dashes, brackets, and parentheses in the following sentences. You may also need to add, delete, or change other marks of punctuation. If a sentence is already correct, write C.

Example 1. In *Incidents in the Life of a Slave Girl* (it was published in 1861), Harriet Ann Jacobs describes the suffering of enslaved women.

21. June and Angies project is a highly detailed analysis of the voting patterns that resulted in the ex mayors defeat.

22. "In America, Edgar Allan Poe [1809–1849] was long regarded as a minor writer, an author of melodramatic poems such as 'The Raven' and 'Annabel Lee' and thrilling tales of mystery and suspense such as 'The Fall of the House of Usher' and 'The Tell-Tale Heart.'"

23. Weve just returned from a trip to the Southwest, where we saw some of Maria Martinezs particularly well crafted pottery.

24. *Freedom's Journal*, which was established in New York City in 1827, was the first newspaper in the United States published by African Americans.

25. Philosopher George Santayana 1863–1952 said, "Those who cannot remember the past are doomed to fulfil (*sic*) it."

26. Indonesia—see the map on page 119—comprises more than 13,500 islands in Southeast Asia, and it's population is the worlds fourth largest.

27. Mrs. Meyers plan is to review everyones portfolio by the end of this week.

28. What you need is a part time job a way to pay your' bills.

29. I need to buy a present for my brother-in-laws birthday; its next Monday.

30. For several years in the 1960's, Zubin Mehta conducted both the Montreal Symphony Orchestra and the Los Angeles Symphony. (don't you recognize his name?)

31. In one recent survey, a four fifths majority of the three hundred sixty five people interviewed supported campaign finance reform.

32. Both my uncle and my father earned their B.A.s at Morehouse College, one of the Atlanta University Centers world famous colleges and universities.

33. The French phrase *je ne sais quoi* [literally, "I do not know what"] refers to a quality that is hard to describe.

34. Doesnt this turkey look oh, no, the cat must have gotten up on the counter!

35. Its anyones' guess whos' responsible for the spray painted *X*s on the three cars windows.

36. Sarahs not going to be able to meet us until one oclock Saturday afternoon.

37. By the time I asked her, shed already promised to take her youngest sisters Brownie troop swimming that morning.

38. The manager replied, "She (the salesclerk who waited on you) is no longer with this company."

39. You should have seen the look on my parents faces when I showed them all the *A*s on my report card.

40. In my opinion, that rabble rousing talk radio commentators antiintellectual stance is just a ploy for duping his audience into accepting the half truths he spouts.

     ELEMENTS OF LANGUAGE | Fifth Course

Spelling: Improving Your Spelling

A. **RECOGNIZING AND CORRECTING MISSPELLED WORDS** Underline the misspelled word in each of the following groups. Then, on the line provided, write the word correctly.

Example 1. amplifying, trampled, <u>decieve</u> _____ *deceive* _____

1. videos, mispeak, stealthily _____

2. silliness, admireable, unwieldy _____

3. turkies, has-beens, counterfeit _____

4. preview, illogical, usualy _____

5. sorely, procede, occurred _____

6. shareing, accede, regrettable _____

7. steadily, acquittal, happyness _____

8. embodyment, immaterial, ninth _____

9. paid, whining, dissapprove _____

10. erasable, disobeyed, referrence _____

11. unecessary, frugally, redeemed _____

12. fortunate, lazyly, mischief _____

13. repairred, lying, frenzied _____

14. receipt, theif, either _____

15. supplied, favored, arguement _____

B. **FORMING THE PLURALS OF NOUNS** On the line provided, write the plural form of each of the following words.

Example 1. hoof _____ *hooves* _____

16. donkey _____

17. *i* _____

18. piano _____

19. comedy _____

20. hand-me-down _____

21. mouse _____

22. coach _____

23. Hillary _____

24. potato _____

25. phenomenon _____

26. self _____

27. box _____

28. Ph.D. _____

29. canary _____

30. radio _____

C. PROOFREADING SENTENCES FOR SPELLING ERRORS For each of the following sentences, underline each misspelled or incorrectly used word or numeral. Above it, write the correct word or numeral.

        shelves four   *nineteen*
Example 1. Each of the <u>shelfs</u> is <u>4</u> feet long and <u>ninteen</u> inches deep.

31. The 1st moveable type was made by Bi Sheng, a Chinese printer, nearly 1,000 years ago.

32. On the 6 o'clock weather report on Channel Five this evening, the meteorologist is predictting

  up to 6 inchs of snow tonight.

33. It may seem hard to beleive, but the human body is approximatly sixty-five percent water.

34. 365 days is normaly the length of a calendar year; in leap years, however, February twenty-

  nine is added to the calendar.

35. We've payed less for gas this month because our new car has been geting forty miles per

  gallon.

D. DISTINGUISHING BETWEEN WORDS OFTEN CONFUSED For each of the following sentences, underline the correct word of the choices in parentheses.

Example 1. Ragweed pollen (*born, borne*) by the wind is responsible for most cases of hay fever

     in the United States.

36. The Pleasant Valley Little Theater's production of Stephen Sondheim's *Anyone Can Whistle* is

  (*all together, altogether*) enjoyable and entertaining.

37. The (*to, too, two*) candidates took part in a televised debate last night.

38. Unfortunately, (*their, there, they're*) debate deteriorated into a shouting match.

39. Newly elected to the city (*consul, council, counsel*), Ms. Abeyto described herself as "jubilant."

40. We are (*all ready, already*) making plans for next year's homecoming parade.

41. "Be careful not to (*loose, lose*) track of the time; the bus will return to the hotel promptly at

  four o'clock," cautioned our tour guide.

42. The state cabinet meets weekly in Room 612 of the (*capital, capitol*).

43. The new members of the National Honor Society will be (*formally, formerly*) inducted at a schoolwide assembly this afternoon.

44. (*Lead, Led*) by the drum major, the band marched onto the football field for the halftime show.

45. The dry soil and scarce moisture of a (*desert, dessert*) make it inhospitable for many forms of plant life.

46. In 1987 Oscar Arias Sánchez of Costa Rica was honored by the Nobel Prize committee for his leadership in bringing (*peace, piece*) to Central America.

47. Almost everyone enjoys receiving a sincere (*complement, compliment*).

48. As we drove (*passed, past*) our old house, we waved to the people on the front porch.

49. Jan Ernst Matzeliger invented an (*ingenious, ingenuous*) machine for attaching the upper part of a shoe to the sole.

50. Does anyone know (*who's, whose*) calculator this is?

Correcting Common Errors

A. CORRECTING USAGE ERRORS IN SENTENCES   Each of the following sentences contains at least one error in usage. Draw a line through the incorrect word or words in each sentence. If a correction needs to be inserted, write the correct word or words above each error.

Example 1. Remind ~~whomever's~~ *whoever's* in charge of refreshments to ~~have included~~ *include* sugar-free snacks.

1. A mirage is a type of optical illusion where an object appears to be closer then it actually is or appears to be real but is not.

2. I wish I would of knowed that Ming Liang and them were carpooling to the concert.

3. Mr. Hernandez, along with his wife and their children, have done a real great job fixing up that old house.

4. Cheering loudly for the home team, the umpire cautioned the crowd not to have ventured onto the field.

5. The bus lurched sudden when the driver swerved to avoid a dog what was laying in the road.

6. Grandpa Higgins showed Jill and I some of the sketches he drawed when he was in Guam.

7. If the security guard don't rise any objections, let's set on the front steps of the courthouse to watch the parade.

8. Pablo and me are going hiking at Indiana Dunes State Park on Saturday.

9. In my opinion, your group's skit was more funnier than any skit on the program.

10. At the Midland Mall they will be hosting the Fairview Watercolor Society's annual show this weekend.

11. When I talk to her on the telephone this morning, Mitzi sounded like she had a cold.

12. Bringing their new baby home from the hospital, the first-time parents raised several times during the night to check on her.

13. If I was you, I'd price them boots at several other stores.

14. We can't afford no digital camera; beside, none of us uses the camera we have.

15. The winner of the debate between Luis and Amelia will be the person who the panel of judges award the most points.

16. This here book on the Incas explains that they weaved cloth from cotton and wool.

17. The thirsty dog stared forlorn at its water dish, which was near empty.

18. Reggie's trumpet solo at last night's concert received more applause than Jack.

19. Because of the holiday, there's less bus routes operating today.

20. Sally and myself seen James Earl Jones's first movie, *Dr. Strangelove,* on television last night.

21. Physics fascinate my stepfather as much as me.

22. Mrs. Williams said during rehearsal us chorus members sung beautiful.

23. Most of the motels near the convention center was full by the time that us delegates tried to make reservations.

24. Having gotten the upgrade of that software, the old version seems so slow now.

25. One way to remember the names of the Great Lakes more easier are to use the acronym HOMES as a mnemonic device.

B. CORRECTING MECHANICS ERRORS IN SENTENCES Each of the following sentences contains at least one error in capitalization, punctuation, or spelling. Draw a line through each error in capitalization and spelling, and write the correct letter or word in the space above the error. In some cases you will need to add or delete punctuation. Underline any words that should be in italics.

Example 1. ~~Its~~ hard to ~~beleive~~ but more than two thousand ~~specieses~~ of freshwater fish live in the Amazon ~~river.~~
(handwritten corrections: It's, believe,, species, R)

26. Well if your absolutely positive that you can't go hiking with us you can be sure that youll be greatly missed

27. Kangaroo and koala are just two of the words, that british settlers in Australia borrowed from the Aboriginal people of that Continent

28. In the United states November 11, the anniversary of the day that World War I 1914–1918 ended is set aside as a day to remember all of our nations' veterans

29. "If you have time after supper, dad would you spend a few minutes quizing me on this material for my History class" Bao asked

30. in Norse mythology Thor was the God of thunder and lightning his hammer which was his primary weapon was called Mjollnir

31. My oldest sister Maria is studying Anthropology at Morningside college in Sioux city Iowa

32. According to this article in the encyclopedia 2 iron oxides in the soil account for the spectacularly beautyful colors of the Painted dessert in Arizona hematite and limonite

33. An imaginary line the Arctic circle delineates an area, where the sun doesn't rise on Winter's shortest day, and doesn't set on summer's longest day

34. "Gail Fred asked, Are you familiar with the book This Land is My Land by George Littlechild

35. The following products are manufacturred in Ecuador cement, processed foods, panama hats, and textiles

36. What i wanted to ask you was oh forget it

37. Pleased principle Morales praised the efforts of the dedicated hardworking teachers

38. The juniors, who have signed up for the class trip to Washington d.c, should pick up thier information packets in Ms Shapiro's office no later than Friday April 3

39. My parents have ordered a new Ford ranger and they are planing to let me have our old Dodge Truck.

40. Three-fourths of the seventy five students I surveyed correctly named the 1st Asian American Olympic gold medalist in figure skating it was Kristi Yamaguchi

41. By the way you might want to revaluate the introduction to your report, it could be livelyer I think

42. Somebodys' car alarm went off at about 3 oclock this morning, and woke my Mom and me from a sound sleep

43. "What a fiasco our trip to that world famous ski resort in Colorado turned out to be' Hal exclaimed!

44. Dolores and i had quiet a lengthy discussion about our differring interpretations of one of argentine writer Jorge Luis Borges' highly-original short stories

45. While your at the store please pick up a copy of the latest issue of Newsweek

46. My guidance councillor Mrs Melrose asked me how many colleges I had applied to?

47. In it's latest promotional package, the bank refered to an enclosed brochure as 'An example of our continuing effort to serve you'. [It (the brochure) was a list of the banks' new higher fees.]

48. The salad contained, lettuce and tomatos and carrots and green onions: it was served with low fat french dressing

49. Edwina explained. "Among the many spirituals that the noted, African American singer and composer Harry Thacker Burleigh arranged was Nobody Knows the Trouble Ive Seen".

50. Did Dr Shimamoto actualy say, I'd like you to try an over the counter medication first, however if that doesnt work, Ill consider prescribing something stronger?"

Writing Clear Sentences

COORDINATING AND SUBORDINATING IDEAS

DIRECTIONS Combine the sentences in each item. You may need to add, delete or rearrange some words. Make your corrections in the space between the lines. Use the heading above each set of sentences to guide you.

Example Bill Phillips wrote *Body for Life*, ~~*Body for Life*~~ explains a strength program.
              ↑ which

Coordinating Ideas

1. Water covers over 70 percent of Earth's surface. Most of Earth's water is undrinkable salt water.

2. Water makes up most of the human body. The brain is mostly made of water. The blood is mostly water. The muscles are mostly water.

3. Eating fast food contributes to weight gain. Avoiding exercise causes people to gain weight.

4. Vitamins are necessary for a healthy life. People also need minerals to stay healthy.

5. My friends who have met Andrea like her. My friends who have met Andrea envy her.

Subordinating Ideas

6. Scientists have studied the brain cells in the hippocampus. The hippocampus is the area of the brain associated with memory.

7. Chiles come in more than three thousand different varieties. The varieties range from very hot to sweet.

8. Seven-month-old dogs can be difficult to control. After reaching seven months, they are no longer dependent on their owners for protection and guidance.

9. My brother loves science fiction novels. He reads a book every night.

10. Senator Witte will not run for reelection. She will run if she gets enough money.

ACHIEVING CLARITY

DIRECTIONS Faulty coordination and faulty parallelism make some of the following sentences confusing. Some items contain fragments or run-ons. Using the methods you have learned, revise each item. You may need to add, delete, or rearrange words. Use the heading above each set of items to guide you. Make your corrections in the space between the lines.

Example   After my car broke down/I had to take it to the shop.

Correcting Faulty Coordination

11. Poor diet choices can cause cholesterol levels to rise, and high cholesterol levels may increase the risk of heart attack.

Using Parallel Structure

12. To carry out a promise is sometimes more difficult than making a promise.

13. He thought that we would attend a lecture and eating a meal.

Revising Phrase Fragments

14. After the Boston Tea Party. The British Parliament passed the Intolerable Acts. A set of laws.

15. I visited an employment agency and my school counselor. To better understand job application forms.

16. Watching television shows, one after another, hour after hour. Some young people forget their responsibilities.

Revising Subordinate Clause Fragments

17. Where a museum of her work has been established. Georgia O'Keeffe painted many scenes of New Mexico.

18. Because we have not had a block party in a long time. My street neighbors want to plan a block party.

Revising Run-on Sentences

19. Flash flooding creates dangerous conditions rain falls too quickly to be absorbed into the ground or to drain.

20. Lasagna, a baked dish, usually consists of layers of boiled lasagna pasta, tomato sauce, cheese, and meat lasagna can also be made with spinach instead of meat.

REVISING A PASSAGE

DIRECTIONS   The following passage needs to be revised. The parts that need
revision are underlined. Use what you have learned to revise the passage in
the following ways:
- Coordinate ideas
- Subordinate ideas
- Correct faulty parallelism
- Correct fragments

Example   Filming in black and white is an art. You have to get the lighting

just right to create depth.

(Example shows handwritten edit: inserting "because" replacing the period between "art" and "You")

It's Wonderful

Everyone should see *It's a Wonderful Life* at least once. I even think it

should be viewed in the original black-and-white format.

The movie entertains almost any audience with its humor. **(21)** Even

sophisticates cannot help but enjoy the moment. When Mary Hatch and

George Bailey fall into the swimming pool beneath the dance floor. **(22)** The

movie includes not only amusing scenes. Dramatic ones as well.

At a pivotal point in the movie, George is summoned home following his

father's heart attack. **(23)** Rather than pursuing his dreams and travel around

the world, George chooses to stay in Bedford Falls and help his family. Later,

at a difficult point in his life, he has second thoughts about his choice and

stands on a bridge looking down at the angry water below. **(24)** Comedy and

drama intertwine with the sudden appearance of Clarence. George's guardian

angel. His clothing and speech are humorously at odds with the "angelic."

However, Clarence shows George what Bedford Falls would be like if George

had never been born. As a result, George learns how influential he has been in

the lives of many others. **(25)** The scene of George asking for his life back is so

touching. Audiences shed tears.

The film's humor and drama make it a classic. See it if you get the chance.

Combining Sentences

COMBINING SENTENCES EFFECTIVELY

DIRECTIONS Combine the sentences in each item. You may have to delete, rearrange, or add words. Make your corrections in the space between the lines. Use the headings above each set of sentences to guide you.

                  intently

Example The bird sat and watched the bug. ~~The bird watched intently.~~

Inserting Single-Word Modifiers and Prepositional Phrases

1. Matt snowboarded down the steep slope. His snowboarding was careful.

2. Dad prepared chicken. Dad prepared the chicken with teriyaki sauce and pineapple.

3. On the northern shore of Great Salt Lake, Robert Smithson created *Spiral Jetty*. Robert Smithson created it with over six thousand tons of material.

Inserting Participial and Absolute Phrases

4. LouAnn was frustrated with her project. LouAnn flung her materials across the table.

5. The family had traveled a great distance. The Morris relatives celebrated the homecoming with a week-long reunion.

Inserting Appositive Phrases

6. Augustine Washington was George Washington's father. He died when George was ten.

Coordinating Ideas

7. Lined up like boxcars, the traffic inches along. Flashing taillights signal the lurching stops and starts.

8. The computer is equipped with a USB port. The printer is equipped with a serial port.

Subordinating Ideas

9. The storm blew into town, tossing shingles, trash cans, and children's toys to nearby yards. I found my plastic water bottle wedged between two boards of a fence.

10. Chris's personality traits make him a pleasure to work with. Chris's personality traits include creativity, enthusiasm, and integrity.

COMBINING SENTENCES FOR STYLE

DIRECTIONS Combine the sentences in each item. You may have to delete, rearrage, or add words. Make your corrections in the space between the lines.

Example   ~~The campers watched~~ the lake, ~~The~~ campers saw the trout.
                    Watching ^   ^ *the*
              ^   ^

11. The bulbs are tulip bulbs. The bulbs are planted six inches below the surface of the ground.

12. We were surprised by some Grammy Awards. The awards recognized new musical artists.

13. The music is for guitar. The music is marked with *V*'s. The *V*'s indicate when to strum.

14. Franklin Delano Roosevelt is known as FDR. FDR held the office of President. The President

    declared war on Japan.

15. Édouard Manet never exhibited with the impressionists. The impressionists considered Manet

    their unofficial leader.

16. Frédéric Chopin played the piano. Frédéric Chopin was a nineteenth-century composer.

    Frédéric Chopin was Polish.

17. Glutathione occurs in plant tissues and glutathione occurs in animal tissues. Glutathione helps

    the body in oxidation-reduction processes.

18. Benjamin Franklin helped Thomas Paine immigrate to the colonies. Thomas Paine wrote

    Common Sense. Common Sense presented arguments for colonial independence.

19. Susan Feniger is a chef. Mary Sue Milliken is a chef. The chefs prepared spicy food on a

    television show. They are two of the authors of the cookbook *Mexican Cooking for Dummies*.

20. The *Iliad* descended from oral tradition. The *Odyssey* descended from oral tradition. Homer

    is credited with organizing the two stories in the written form known today.

REVISING A PASSAGE

DIRECTIONS The following passage contains sentences that need to be improved. The parts that need to be improved are underlined. Use what you have learned to revise the passage in the following ways:

- Insert phrases
- Coordinate ideas
- Subordinate ideas

Example I gave up baby-sitting,ₐ*after* I took a job as a horse trainer.

The Pleasures and Trials of Baby-sitting

When I was about twelve years old, I overheard my neighbor,
Mrs. Pulman, say, **(21)** <u>"I couldn't survive without the help of my baby sitter.
My baby sitter is practically my right hand."</u> To know that she appreciated
the many afternoons and Saturday nights I had spent caring for her children
made me feel good. Looking back, I realize that baby-sitting had both advantages and disadvantages for me.

My baby-sitting business grew and provided me with several benefits.
I acquired the reputation of being responsible and reliable. People like
Mrs. Pulman recommended me to other families. However, making money
was the best part. I always had cash in my pocket. **(22)** <u>I didn't have to ask
my parents for advances. These advances were made on my allowance.</u>
Whenever a friend had a birthday, I could buy a gift. If I wanted to get something at the mall or go to a movie, I would. Just about any time I found myself
short of cash, I could find a baby-sitting job. I liked all of these advantages.

Nevertheless, I have begun to see the downside of baby-sitting. **(23)** <u>I made
a lot of money. I did not save very much of it.</u> After all that time and work, I
had only two hundred dollars. How was I going to pay for college? I also realized that I had no other job experience. **(24)** <u>My friends had held jobs at the
mall. They worked as interns for local businesses.</u> I had only fed children,
changed diapers, and watched countless episodes of my favorite sitcoms.
Another unpleasant surprise awaited me when I got a "real" job: taxes and
insurance were taken out of my check. As a baby sitter, I had missed some
important lessons.

While I was baby-sitting, I reaped the rewards work can bring. However,
I did not understand the value of money and I wasted a lot of what I made.
Now I am watching my budget and saving a portion of my weekly check.
(25) <u>None of us can change the past. We can learn from it.</u>

Improving Sentence Style

VARYING SENTENCE BEGINNINGS

DIRECTIONS   Revise each of the following sentences by varying sentence beginnings. Make your corrections in the space between the lines. Use the heading above each set of sentences to guide you.

Example   *On Dr. Seuss's birthday,* ̭My little sister's class dressed in costume ~~because they were~~ ⊙

~~honoring Dr. Seuss on his birthday~~

Single-word Modifier First

1. The runner grabbed the water and drank it quickly.

2. The stuffed bunny looked worn and dingy as it lay on the bed.

Prepositional Phrase First

3. The grass and flowers grow quite well in the backyard.

4. Sometimes my brother and I get bored on long weekends and holidays.

Participial Phrase First

5. The quarterback felt frustrated by the incomplete passes and asked for a timeout.

6. People clapped and cheered and rose to their feet after the performance.

Infinitive Phrase First

7. You smash avocado and mix it with tomatoes, onion, and seasoning to make guacamole.

8. Simira studies, participates in class, and completes assignments to earn an A.

Adverb Clause Modifier First

9. The shoppers deliberated about their purchases because the makeup shelves displayed a

   rainbow of nail colors.

10. College applicants request application packages after they identify the colleges they want

    to attend.

VARYING SENTENCE STRUCTURE AND REDUCING WORDINESS

DIRECTIONS Combine the sentences in each item. You may have to delete, add, or rearrange words. Remember what you have learned about varying sentence beginnings and sentence structures as well as reducing wordiness. Make your corrections in the space between the lines.

Example ~~Many~~ people ~~were~~ (horrified by the volcanic eruption) ~~and~~ evacuated.

11. You must know where your money goes to balance a budget. You must watch every dollar you spend.

12. If Carlton has picked out the music, it could be challenging. It probably will be.

13. A new movie stages its debut this fine evening at the cinema house in the heart of the city.

14. Our prom will be called "Dancing the Night Away." Our prom will be held at the mall.

15. I am excited about getting my driver's license. I am nervous about getting my driver's license. I will take the driver's license test tomorrow.

16. A new job provides many experiences for a teenager. A new job provides many responsibilities for a teenager.

17. By means of dropping the atomic bomb, the U.S. defeated Japan. The U.S. dropped two atomic bombs on Japan during World War II.

18. A student can learn to analyze poetry by examining a poem's structure. A student can learn to analyze poetry by examining a poem's content. A student can learn to analyze poetry by examining a poem's diction.

19. Carlos Santana had been participating in the music industry for many years. Santana won eight awards at the 42nd Grammy Awards.

20. Technology begins changing as quickly as it is produced. Technology keeps consumers constantly upgrading their products.

REVISING A PASSAGE

DIRECTIONS Revise the paragraphs below. The parts that need to be improved are underlined. As you revise, remember to vary sentence beginnings and sentence structure and to eliminate wordiness. Make your corrections in the space between the lines.

                    As a child
Example ~~In the days of his extreme youth~~, he hid under the covers and read
                  ^
            books by flashlight.

Book Look

It happened again last night. The clock chimed 2:00 A.M. Once again I had been reading long past bedtime, but it was worth it! If only everyone could experience the thrill of connecting with a good book.

Sometimes a book is a page-turner. **(21)** <u>Readers get absorbed in the central conflict. They cannot put the book down.</u> They want to find out what will happen next. **(22)** <u>Even young children can experience this kind of excitement when they examine words closely to comprehend what the words are saying.</u>

Often a page-turner will tell the story of a particular character that the reader comes to know as a friend. **(23)** <u>The relationship becomes strong. The reader devours the book in one night.</u> No sooner is the book finished than the reader heads to the library or bookstore, hoping to find another book about that new friend. **(24)** <u>The reader discovers that no other book about the character is available. The reader looks for other books written by the author or for books written about the author.</u> If none can be found, the reader desperately searches for another book in the same genre.

Book lovers constantly gather new information about books and their authors. **(25)** <u>They ask friends what they are reading. They ask family members what they are reading.</u> They seek out the public librarian to find out what is new and what titles they have missed. Avid readers cannot wait until the next time an early morning hour catches them engrossed in a good book.

Understanding Paragraphs and Compositions

DIRECTIONS Read the paragraphs below. Then use what you have learned about paragraph structure to write answers to the items next to the paragraphs.

EXAMPLE

Our backyard becomes a swamp whenever we get a lot of rain. In fact, last spring it rained so much we not only had standing water, but enough of it to launch little plastic boats. It was quite a sight.

1. Write one transition word or phrase used in this paragraph.
  in fact

Paragraph 1

Another reason I believe in teen curfews is my concern for teens' safety. For example, teens who stay out late must either drive or walk home when they are tired, when visibility is limited, and when crime rates are statistically high. Therefore, the curfews help parents and communities ensure the well-being of their young people. I do disagree with some of the traditional consequences for violating a curfew, especially those that punish parents rather than teens. Teen curfews can help protect young people while allowing them enough freedom to practice important decision-making skills.

Paragraph 2

I'll never forget the day Scott introduced me to his pet—a charming and furry ferret. Scott was dedicated to preserving them and had been writing to politicians urging them to pass legislation friendly to this cause. Because of Scott's efforts, black-footed ferrets would no longer lack supporters. Little Finigan lived a pampered, domesticated life, but, according to Scott, his relatives, the black-footed ferrets, were on the Endangered and Threatened Mammal Species list. Frankly, I thought he should just visit them with Finigan on a leash.

PARAGRAPH 1

1. Underline the topic sentence.

2. Circle the transition words.

3. Cross out the sentence that detracts from the unity of the paragraph.

PARAGRAPH 2

4. Number the sentences in this paragraph to show the most logical order.

5. What is the main idea of this paragraph?

_____

_____

6. Underline the clincher sentence.

DIRECTIONS The following passage needs to be revised. Use what you have learned about paragraphs and compositions to answer the items in the right column.

For the Record

Few Americans realize that the British were not the first Europeans to establish a permanent settlement in what would become the United States. Captain John Smith (Jamestown, 1607) and Miles Standish (Plymouth, 1620) are famous names. Why have so few people heard of Pedro Menéndez de Avilés?

After being commissioned, de Avilés left Spain in July of 1565 with eleven ships and nearly two thousand men. In August, he sailed into the bay of St. Augustine. The colony he founded, now the city of St. Augustine, is the oldest continuously occupied European settlement in the United States. De Avilés also explored the Atlantic and Gulf Coasts of what is now Florida and constructed forts. King Philip II of Spain commissioned de Avilés to drive out the French and to establish a Spanish colony in Florida. As governor of Florida, he led the colony until his death in 1574. Unlike other colonial founders, de Avilés's name is not well known. Yet his extraordinary leadership and determination ensured the long-term success of St. Augustine.

The Spanish deserve credit for establishing the first European colony in the United States. Perhaps a future celebration will include the founding of St. Augustine by Pedro Menéndez de Avilés.

7. Which technique is used to introduce this short article—addressing the reader directly, an interesting quotation, a question or challenge, an anecdote?

_____

8. Use the paragraph symbol (¶) to show where a new paragraph should begin.

9. Circle three of the direct references in the second paragraph. (Only one should be a pronoun.)

10. Circle the sentence that is not in chronological order, and draw an arrow to show where it should be placed.

DIRECTIONS The following passage needs to be revised. Use what you have learned about paragraphs and compositions to answer the items in the right column.

Is There Anything to Battle Between the Sexes?

Men Are From Mars, Women Are From Venus claims the title of a book that focuses on relationships between the sexes. Relationship counselor John Gray focuses on the differences between men and women to help the two sexes understand each other. However, are men and women really that different? Have you noticed, for instance, the similarities between men's and women's magazines?

For example, fashion interests both men and women. What's in style and what's not gets a large share of the text and graphics in both types of magazines. Everything from shoes and accessories to suits and sportswear shows up in both men's and women's magazines. In addition, articles and advertisements on skin-care, a topic traditionally considered a feminine interest, appear in men's magazines. Wrinkles increase with age because the skin loses elasticity as people age. Both men's and women's magazines carry personal improvement articles focusing on relationships, careers, self-esteem and help with technology. In addition, the price of magazines has increased dramatically in the last ten years. Other articles that interest men and women focus on athletes and celebrities. Both men's and women's magazines feature stories on track heroes, weight lifters, soccer players, movie stars, and television personalities. An examination of the topics covered in men's and women's magazines reveals that men's and women's interests are similar. Take a look at a general interest magazine for the opposite sex the next time you have a chance. You may find that men and women do not hail from different planets. You may learn that the sexes have a lot in common.

topic sentence for the second paragraph: _____

_____

11. Which technique is used to introduce this short article—a dramatic quotation, a question or challenge, an anecdote, a stand on a hot issue?

_____

_____

12. Cross out the two sentences that destroy the unity of the piece.

13. Use the paragraph symbol (¶) to show where a new paragraph should begin.

14. Write a topic sentence for the second paragraph.

15. Which of these techniques is used in the conclusion—referring to the introduction, offering a solution, summarizing major points, restating the thesis? Explain your answer.

_____

_____

_____

_____

Reading Workshop: Autobiographical Narrative

DIRECTIONS Read the following passage, and answer the questions in the right-hand column.

An Unlikely Path

Some people claim that they have known from childhood what their life's calling is. Not until the fall of my sophomore year in college did I realize what I really wanted to do with my life. I do not owe this realization to keen personal insight or a riveting revelation, but to a simple creature who stumbled into my life one crisp October afternoon.

The sun that day was still bright as it dodged behind trees and began its descent to the horizon. The bite of autumn made me walk with a mixed feeling of contentment and restlessness. With my mind in a daze, I didn't see the tan-and-black-spotted shaggy mutt following me. I finally noticed the little fellow when he playfully swatted my leg with his wagging tail. He had a raggedy beard and bushy eyebrows that seemed to rise in anticipation when I bent down to pet his head.

"Go home, Shaggy," I told him. He didn't listen, and kept following me until I arrived at the intersection of Columbus and Elwood, a block away from my apartment. I crossed the street.

Interested in a bag of food scraps lying next to the corner wire wastebasket, he paused at the curb and stayed behind to investigate the remaining tidbits. His tail wagging vigorously, he buried his nose in the greasy bag, digging for the treasure that lurked within. I smiled and watched him as he withdrew his wiry snout from the bag, his teeth clenching a bounty of discarded bread and cheese. Eager to show off his loot, he looked up and noticed that I had crossed the street. He bounded onto the pavement to catch up with his newfound friend.

1. What phrases show time order in the first two paragraphs?

_____

_____

_____

_____

2. What kinds of sensory details does the writer include in the second paragraph?

_____

_____

_____

_____

3. What type of details does the writer use to make the fourth paragraph realistic?

_____

_____

_____

_____

"No, stop!" I shouted at the dog when I saw the oncoming car. The screeching sound of the tires and the hard smack of the bumper hitting the dog's side caused every pore on my body to open and flush with adrenaline and shock.

If only I had kept walking, or he had run faster, or he hadn't seen me, I thought frantically as I kneeled over the dog to see if he was still breathing. As he lay there, I brushed his matted hair away from his eyes and cradled his head in my hands. He was still breathing and tried to stand on all fours, but his two back legs lay limp, like broken branches dangling from a tree.

"I'm so sorry, I didn't see your dog. He just bounded out before I could stop," said the driver.

Ten minutes later, the dog and I were in the examination room of an animal clinic. Shaggy had no internal injuries, just a cut on his head and two broken legs.

Because of his injuries, Shaggy would need constant care. Even though he was not my dog, I agreed to pay for his stay at the vet's, and adopt him as my pet. Because I was a few hundred dollars short of the total amount for his bill, I agreed to work three afternoons a week to cover the rest of Shaggy's fees.

During those afternoons at the clinic, my focus changed. Instead of thinking about myself, my interest centered on the animals in the clinic. As each day went by, I grew more anxious to spend time at the clinic, to tend to Shaggy during his recuperation, and to assist the staff with the furry patients. At the end of the semester, I registered for animal anatomy and physiology courses and declared my major: pre-veterinary medicine.

It seems strange that a stray dog led me to my career. Sometimes accidents can lead us to a path we may not otherwise have considered.

4. What thoughts about the accident does the writer include in the sixth paragraph?

_____

_____

_____

_____

_____

5. How does the writer make the driver's reaction realistic?

_____

_____

_____

_____

_____

6. How is the order of events in this narrative organized?

_____

_____

_____

_____

_____

DIRECTIONS Use the ideas and information from the passage you have just read to complete the graphic organizer.

Identifying Narrative and Descriptive Details

▶ NARRATIVE/ DESCRIPTIVE DETAILS	▶ EXAMPLE
1. Specific events and actions	
2. Thoughts and feelings	
3. Figurative language	*"The sun that day was still bright as it dodged behind trees and began its descent to the horizon."*
4. Sensory language	
5. Factual and spatial details	

Writing Workshop: Autobiographical Narrative

DIRECTIONS Use the following guidelines to help you revise and correct the essay on the next page.

THE INTRODUCTION SHOULD

- capture the reader's attention
- provide background information
- hint at the meaning of the experience

THE BODY SHOULD

- vividly portray events, people, and places
- place events in an order that makes sense
- add to the meaning of the autobiographical narrative with each event

THE CONCLUSION SHOULD

- reveal the final outcome
- make the meaning of the experience clear
- draw the paper to a close

REMEMBER TO

- ❏ correct run-on sentences
- ❏ include vivid details

Writing Workshop: Revising and Proofreading

DIRECTIONS The following autobiographical narrative was written in response to this prompt:

Write about a meaningful experience in which you learned something significant about yourself or about life in general.

The narrative contains problems in style, organization, content, and grammar.

- Use the space between the lines to revise the paper and correct the errors.
- If you cannot fit some of your revisions between the lines, rewrite the revised sections on a separate piece of paper.

The Camera Never Lies

"I'll go first," I said when my senior English teacher asked for volunteers to begin the oral presentations. I had been ready for a week. Ever since my sophomore year, I have been prepared for public presentations. I learned the hard way that being unprepared can set you up for embarrassment and disappointment.

That year my television production class produced a daily news report that was broadcast within the school. I also took English, biology, and world history every day. I had taken my turn operating the camera and editing video tapes, and I was finally going to take my turn in front of the camera. I would not only be the star, I would cover sports, the most popular topic of our broadcast. Because I would be on the air for only three minutes, I presumed it would be easy to figure out what to say.

> **a.** Problem with content

I had planned to arrive at school an hour early the morning of my big day to read the paper and write my sports report, but

> **b.** Problem with order

everything went wrong. Each day an hour before class met, the

reporters would read the local paper and decide together which sto-

ries to cover, choosing local and national events along with impor-

tant school-related events. When I finally got to school, I had only

twenty minutes to find a newspaper, write my segment, and get to

class. I barely had time to write a few sentences for my report. I

set my alarm for the wrong time. My dad had taken the newspaper

with him to work.

Before the news program began, Mr. Morgan, the advisor,

reminded me to direct my report to camera two. My moment in the

spotlight had arrived, the problem was that I had only enough

material for a twenty-second report.

> **c.** Problem with run-on sentence

Paul, the student anchor, introduced me. I heard myself say,

"Thanks, Paul," and then say something about our school basketball

team's winning streak. After that, my report progressed in a blur.

I felt the lights on my face. I looked down at my paper and could

barely read what I had written. I reported the score from the soccer

game and the time for that evening's basketball game. Then I had

nothing left to say but, "That's all I have this week. Back to you,

Paul." Fortunately, Paul quickly took up my slack and went into his

next report.

> **d.** Problem with a lack of vivid details

After the broadcast, Paul tried to comfort me, but I just wanted to

hide and never go on camera again.

> **e.** Problem with conclusion

Reading Workshop: Extended Definition

DIRECTIONS Read the following article, and answer the questions in the right-hand column.

What Is Information Literacy?

We live in the Information Age. Since the development of the Internet and the World Wide Web, the avenues for transferring information have dramatically increased. Consequently, the number of sources of information available has multiplied exponentially. Without leaving home, people can find out about the weather on another continent, read breaking news, download a recipe, or play chess with someone half a world away. Accessing this wealth of information requires information literacy, a special kind of knowledge.

Although there are many different types of literacies, they are all related to the same basic definition. *Webster's Dictionary* defines literacy as being able to read and write and having knowledge or competence. Information literacy, then, is the knowledge or competence to access and use information. It is the ability to access a variety of resources, select and evaluate appropriate information, and use it effectively. Another type of literacy is media literacy. Media literacy is focused on the ability of viewers to analyze media.

Information literacy requires two principal types of skills: navigating and evaluating. These skills closely intertwine. A person who is information literate can navigate the Internet and access a variety of resources—including experts available through e-mail and search engines. The skill to navigate the Web is essential considering that finding relevant and reliable sources is one of the most critical steps in writing. When working on a research project, a writer decides what specific information is needed. Based on those needs, the writer determines the most useful place to get information: the

1. What main idea does the author develop in the first two paragraphs?

_____

_____

_____

_____

_____

2. To what larger category does information literacy belong?

_____

_____

_____

_____

_____

3. What details does the writer use to support the main idea of the third paragraph?

_____

_____

_____

_____

_____

library, the Internet, or through e-mail to an expert. Once a writer has found the necessary sources, their validity must be determined through careful evaluation. Finding sources, or navigating the Web, and evaluating those sources are the basic elements of information literacy.

Information literacy is even more important in today's data-rich and technologically driven environment. Not only is a vast amount of information available, it is constantly updated. As information becomes obsolete faster, the person who knows how to use technological resources effectively to find, access, and evaluate the latest news and information will have an advantage.

Regardless of technological developments and societal changes, there will always be something to discover, explain, or solve. Today and in the future, information literacy will continue to be one of the most crucial forms of literacy used on a daily basis. The people who can apply effective navigation and evaluation skills to the Internet and other technologies are the ones who will succeed. Because information literacy will allow them to find resources and select relevant information, these people will have the world at their fingertips.

4. What classification technique does the writer use in the third paragraph?

_____
_____
_____
_____
_____

5. What is the main idea of the fourth paragraph?

_____
_____
_____
_____
_____

DIRECTIONS Use the ideas and information in the passage you have just read to complete the graphic organizer. Identify the methods the writer used to classify "information literacy" by looking for the subject's larger category and the subject's specific characteristics.

Analyzing Classification

CATEGORY   MEMBER   CHARACTERISTICS

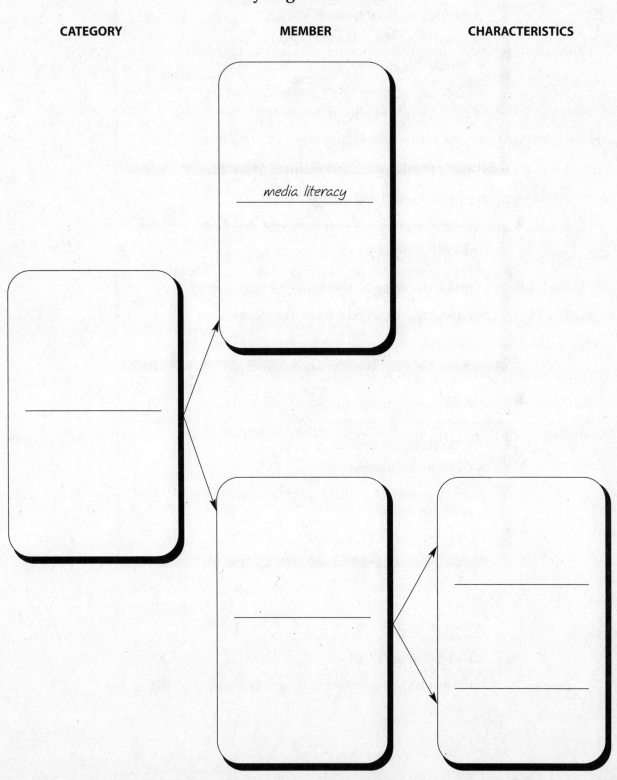

media literacy

Writing Workshop: Extended Definition

DIRECTIONS Use the following guidelines to help you revise and correct the essay on the next page.

THE INTRODUCTION SHOULD

- use an attention-grabbing opening
- identify the term and its category
- supply any necessary background information
- provide a clear thesis

THE BODY SHOULD

- develop the thesis with a variety of examples, illustrations, personal anecdotes, descriptions, or analogies
- present the details in an order that makes sense

THE CONCLUSION SHOULD

- summarize the definition
- briefly explain the importance or relevance of the extended definition

---

REMEMBER TO

- ❑ eliminate lazy qualifiers
- ❑ punctuate essential and nonessential modifiers correctly

Writing Workshop: Revising and Proofreading

DIRECTIONS The following essay was written in response to this prompt:

> **Write an extended definition of a term.**

The essay contains problems in style, content, organization, and grammar.

- Use the space between the lines to revise the essay and correct the errors.
- If you cannot fit some of your revisions between the lines, rewrite the revised sections on a separate piece of paper.

What Is Independence?

We teenagers, who tend to be obsessed with independence, rarely

stop to think about what the term means. When we do, we usually

define it as something someone else gives us. Independence is not

something that comes from outside ourselves, however. We may also

think of independence as the freedom to do anything we want. But

that is not the real meaning of the word either. Independence is a

character trait, that enables an individual to make decisions and act

upon them without placing too much emphasis on the opinion of

others.

> **a.** Problem with punctuating a modifier

Independence means not having to rely on others. We may con-

sider ourselves to be independent when our parents allow us to

drive without adult supervision. That permission is kind of a step

toward some kind of independence. However, those of us who are

merely concerned with where our friends want to go are not really

independent at all. Even though we may be given freedom from our

> **b.** Problems with qualifiers

parents' control, it is also necessary for us to be independent from

the influence of our friends.

Some people define independence as not caring what anyone

else says or thinks. Even the founders who declared this nation

independent were concerned with respecting others' opinions. That

attitude stretches and distorts the true meaning of independence.

There is a difference between relying on one's own abilities and

judgments and being absolutely indifferent to what others think.

c. Problem with order

We must remember that we are not the only ones who can think

or the only ones whose opinions matter. Only then can we learn to

act independently in the best interests of ourselves and others.

d. Problem with conclusion

Reading Workshop: Progress Report

DIRECTIONS Read the following passage, and answer the questions in the right-hand column.

What's the Score: A Progress Report on Title IX

As recently as 1970, Virginia state law prohibited women's admittance to the College of Arts and Sciences at the University of Virginia. About forty years later, women make up the majority of enrolled undergraduates at the university.

What made the difference? A law known as Title IX, modeled on Title VI of the Civil Rights Act of 1964, has had a profound impact on American education. Title IX went into effect in 1972. Its goal was to put an end to sex discrimination in federally assisted education programs. Because almost all schools receive federal assistance, the effects were dramatic. Today, decades after the law's passage, substantial advances in gender equity in education are evident. Yet, there remains further progress to be made.

In 1971, only 18 percent of female high school graduates went on to complete four years of college, compared to 26 percent of male high school graduates. This education gap no longer exists: About 27 percent of both male and female high school graduates earn bachelor's degrees. In addition, the majority of students earning associate's and master's degrees today are women.

Title IX regulations applied to school athletic programs have also dramatically increased women's participation in sports. In 1972, one in twenty-seven high school females participated in organized sports. By 1997, the ratio had risen to one in every three females. At the college level, more than 180,000 women participated in intercollegiate sports in 2006–up from 16,000 in 1970. During this same period, college spending on athletic scholarships for women increased from $100,000 to more than $200 million.

1. What main idea does the first paragraph present?

_____

_____

_____

_____

_____

2. What measurements of progress does the writer cite in the third paragraph?

_____

_____

_____

_____

_____

3. How would you summarize the fourth paragraph?

_____

_____

_____

_____

_____

Chapter Tests

Despite these indications of progress, the gender gap still exists in some areas of education and athletics. Women still earn fewer doctoral degrees than men and fewer professional degrees in fields such as law and medicine. Women are also underrepresented in the studies of science and engineering. On the playing field, females are still less involved in sports than males and also tend to drop out of sports-related activities at earlier ages. At the high school level, boys' varsity teams outnumber girls' teams by 24,000. At the college level, women make up only 37 percent of student athletes and receive only one-third of all athletic scholarships.

Although there is no deadline for when the full benefits and effects of Title IX are to be realized, progress has been made for gender equality in education. The education gap that existed between men and women in completing four years of college has narrowed, and women and girls now participate in athletics in far greater numbers than they did in the past. While these measurements of progress serve to remind us that Title IX is working, total equality in higher education remains a goal for which to aim.

4. What measurements in the fifth paragraph illustrate a lack of progress?

_____

_____

_____

_____

_____

5. How would you summarize this entire progress report?

_____

_____

_____

_____

_____

DIRECTIONS Use the ideas and information in the passage you have just read to complete the graphic organizer.

Analyzing Measurements of Progress

▶ STEPS	▶ EXPLANATION / ANALYSIS
Step 1: Define the goal in the report.	*The progress is toward gender equity in education. The final goal would be complete equity in all aspects of education.*
Step 2: Identify the time frame for completion of the project.	
Step 3: Identify the ways progress has been measured.	
Step 4: Decide how much progress has been made since Title IX was introduced.	
Step 5: Note if the goal is abstract or ideal, and explain why the ideal may never be reached.	

Writing Workshop: Progress Report

DIRECTIONS Use the following guidelines to help you revise and correct the essay on the next page.

THE INTRODUCTION SHOULD

- identify the project
- describe the time period covered
- include the purpose or goal

THE BODY SHOULD

- give background information and define unfamiliar terms
- give evidence and essential information for each accomplishment
- present information in an effective order
- explain any problems

THE CONCLUSION SHOULD

- present an overall view of the project's progress
- confirm or revise the time schedule for completion of the project
- describe future plans

REMEMBER TO

- ❏ vary sentence length
- ❏ use verb tenses correctly

Writing Workshop: Revising and Proofreading

DIRECTIONS The following progress report was written in response to this prompt:

> **Report on the progress of an event or project in which you have been involved.**

This essay contains problems in style, content, organization, and grammar.

- Use the space between the lines to revise the paper and correct the errors.
- If you cannot fit some of your revisions between the lines, rewrite the revised sections on a separate piece of paper.

Progress Report: Delwood High School Book Fair

For some time, the members of the Delwood High School Book

Club have been organizing a book fair to benefit the school library.

The purposes for the book fair are to add books to the library's cur-

rent collection and to provide free books to students.

a. Problem with introduction

The main responsibilities include obtaining book donations,

recruiting volunteers, and creating advertisements. In January, we

brainstormed ideas for adding books to the library with our spon-

sor, Ms. Diaz, the school librarian. Then we divided responsibilities.

We came up with the idea for a book fair, which we thought would

be a fun way for our organization to support the library and help

other students.

b. Problem with order

My responsibility has been to contact local businesses for finan-

cial support and civic groups for book donations. During February, I

contacted eight bookstores, and five offered to donate books. Three

of the stores have already sent their donations to the school.

This week, Karen Dannevik's mother offered to help us promote the book fair. She has agreed to donate one thousand buttons with our logo. We will pick up the buttons a week before the fair. We can pass them out to students a week before the fair.

> **c.** Problem with sentence length

Our only remaining problem is finding enough student volunteers. Because our school requires one hundred hours of community service by graduation, we hoped that more students would volunteer in return for community service credit.

> **d.** Problem with verb tense

We still need to organize the books, train the volunteers we have, and distribute flyers. Media advertising will begin next week, and over the weekend we will hang the posters. I am proud that our organization has been able to make our idea work so far.

> **e.** Problem with conclusion

Reading Workshop: Problem-Solution Article

DIRECTIONS Read the following article, and answer the questions in the right-hand column.

On the Road to Clean Air: Alternative Solutions

One of our most valuable natural resources is something we need every minute of every day—air. However, as our economy and society have developed, so has air pollution.

In the United States, 60 percent of all air pollution comes from car exhaust. Car fumes contain chemicals that react with sunlight to produce three hazards: ozone, the main ingredient in smog; carbon dioxide, a contributor to global warming; and tiny particles of ash and soot that pollute the environment. Although catalytic converters (required since 1970) have decreased emissions, more people in the United States are driving cars. During a recent study, drivers clocked three trillion miles, an increase of 127 percent over the last thirty years. Past efforts to limit toxic pollutants may not be sufficient to counteract the huge increase in the number of cars on the road. What is the solution to this problem?

In response to this problem, the Environmental Protection Agency (EPA) has issued a set of tough rules designed to reduce the tailpipe emissions from new passenger cars and light trucks. These standards accompany requirements for reduced sulfur levels in fuel nationwide. The EPA estimates that this program will ensure cleaner air by reducing vehicle emissions to a level equivalent to removing 166 million cars from the road.

1. What problem can you infer from the title of the article?

_____
_____
_____
_____
_____

2. According to the first paragraph, what is the central problem?

_____
_____
_____
_____
_____

3. What ideas in the second paragraph present an extended description of the problem?

_____
_____
_____
_____
_____

Another promising solution is the arrival of "clean cars." These battery-powered electric cars and hybrid cars that run on a combination of electricity and low-sulfur gasoline may offer consumers an attractive option for reducing air pollution. The Environmental Defense Fund has stated that each electric vehicle driven in Los Angeles would contribute 49 to 66 percent less carbon dioxide per mile than a gasoline-powered vehicle. Battery-powered cars, however, are limited in the number of miles they can cover without being recharged, and the cost of most electric or hybrid cars is higher than the initial cost of a conventional car of the same size.

Automakers are also expecting to mass produce cars that use hydrogen instead of gas or electricity. These vehicles could reduce air pollution and, at the same time, create a new energy economy based on the extraction of hydrogen as a fuel source. Another advantage to a hydrogen-burning fuel cell is that it is long lasting— the electrical current never dies as long as the cell has fuel. However, these cars are not widely available to the general public.

The reliance on automobiles in the United States has created an air pollution problem and increased the need for alternative ways to ease pollution. While the EPA's regulations and recent developments in fuel-efficient cars address the air-pollution problem, these efforts might not offer long-term solutions. The best long-term solution to ensuring clean air and a healthier environment may be to eliminate dependence on fossil fuel altogether. Finding an energy alternative to fossil fuel may be one of the greatest challenges facing this generation.

4. What solution is discussed in the fourth paragraph?

_____

_____

_____

_____

_____

5. Which solution do you think has the greatest possibility of success? Why?

_____

_____

_____

_____

_____

DIRECTIONS Use the ideas and information from the passage you have just read to complete the graphic organizer.

Identifying the Implied Main Idea

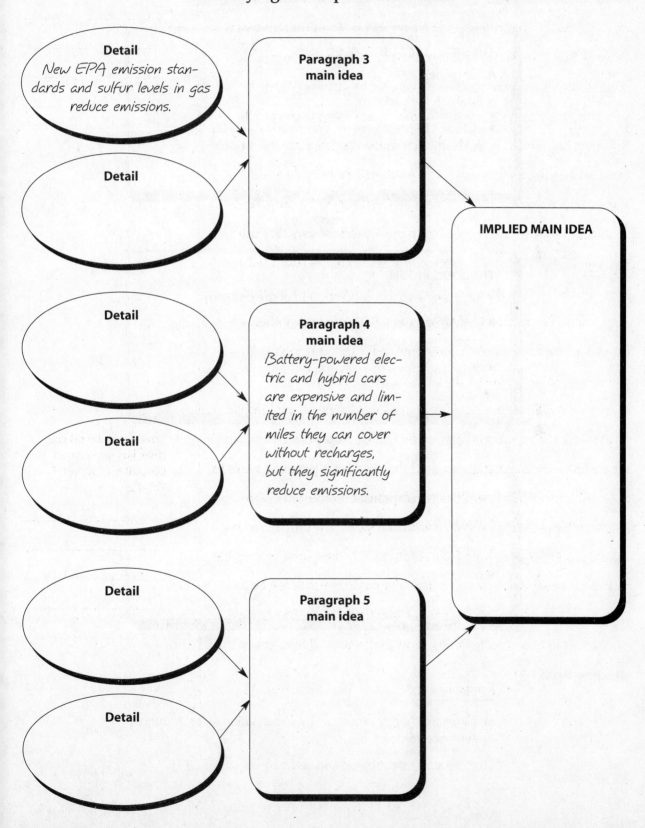

Detail
New EPA emission standards and sulfur levels in gas reduce emissions.

Detail

Paragraph 3 main idea

Detail

Detail

Paragraph 4 main idea
Battery-powered electric and hybrid cars are expensive and limited in the number of miles they can cover without recharges, but they significantly reduce emissions.

IMPLIED MAIN IDEA

Detail

Detail

Paragraph 5 main idea

Writing Workshop: Problem-Solution Essay

DIRECTIONS Use the following guidelines to help you revise and correct the essay on the next page.

THE INTRODUCTION SHOULD

- get readers interested

- establish the problem

- include a thesis statement that clearly states the problem and mentions solutions

THE BODY SHOULD

- include an expanded description of the problem

- include authoritative and concrete evidence about the problem and solutions

- discuss solutions in a clear, organized way

THE CONCLUSION SHOULD

- restate the problem

- summarize the solutions

- provide an outlook for the future

REMEMBER TO

☐ eliminate choppy sentences by coordinating ideas through sentence combining

☐ make sure that subjects and verbs agree

Writing Workshop: Revising and Proofreading

DIRECTIONS The following problem-solution essay was written in response to this prompt:

What can teenagers do to improve their eating habits?

The essay contains problems in content, style, organization, and grammar.

- Use the space between the lines to revise the paper and correct the errors.
- If you cannot fit some of your revisions between the lines, rewrite the revised sections on a separate piece of paper.

Teen Diets: Learning to Eat Smart

You are running late again and have no time for breakfast at home. Instead, you grab a candy bar from the depths of your back-pack. You do not get really hungry until lunch anyway. A recent study of teen nutritional needs show that continually skipping breakfast, or choosing a candy bar instead of carrots, can have long-term health consequences.

> **a.** Problem with subject-verb agreement

> **b.** Problem with thesis statement

The fact that many teens skip meals means their diets fall far short of providing the essential nutrients needed for this period of rapid growth and development. Often teens do not consume the minimum recommended daily amounts of zinc, iron, and calcium. Zinc is necessary for healthy skin. Zinc is important for emotional stability. Zinc is also crucial in overall growth. Iron is crucial for the development of healthy red blood cells and muscles. Teens also need calcium, which is essential for bone development. Unfortunately, most teenagers eat what is easiest for them to grab instead of what is good for them.

> **c.** Problem with choppy sentences

So what healthy options do busy teenagers have? At lunch, teens should avoid the snack line and, instead, find out what healthful choices the school cafeteria provides. In the evenings, when teens have more time, they should try to eat plenty of fresh fruits and vegetables. Many cafeterias offer salads with low-calorie dressing, grilled chicken sandwiches, or baked potatoes. In between meals, instead of grabbing candy bars, teens should choose high protein snacks like granola bars or sunflower seeds. If teens are in a rush in the morning, they can grab a piece of fruit or a calcium-rich snack like yogurt or cheese and eat it on the way to school.

d. Problem with organization

There are some key ways teenagers can overcome poor eating habits and learn to make nutritional choices that will keep them healthy throughout their lives.

e. Problem with conclusion

Reading Workshop: Literary Analysis of a Novel

DIRECTIONS Read the following passage, and answer the questions in the right-hand column.

The Civil War Below and the Blue Sky Above

"Here they come!" (33) cry the men down the line in Stephen Crane's *The Red Badge of Courage*. Henry Fleming, a young soldier fighting in the Civil War, picks up his rifle. Later, in the moments after the battle's noise and smoke and blood, Henry looks at the sky to get his bearings.

> As he gazed around him the youth felt a flash of astonishment at the blue, pure sky and the sun gleaming on the trees and fields. It was surprising that Nature had gone tranquilly on with her golden process in the midst of so much devilment. (39)

Death and destruction do not affect the sky's blue serenity. As Henry observes the horrors around him in contrast with the beauty above, he realizes that the natural world is indifferent toward the opposing sides in a civil war. He gradually understands that his frantic activity as part of the 304th New York Union regiment— whether as green recruit, frightened deserter, or experienced soldier—has little to do with the larger forces of an unchanging and uncaring, but eminently beautiful Nature.

As a recruit waiting for battle in the seemingly directionless marching, Henry at first believes that the night sky is sympathetic to his experience: "There was a caress in the soft winds; and the whole mood of the darkness, he thought, was one of sympathy for himself in his distress" (17). Homesick and despondent before his first battle, Henry feels as though he will fail as a soldier. The laughter and jokes of the war veterans around him do not relieve his mood. Only the sky, with the "liquid stillness of the night" and the

1. How would you para-phrase the main idea of this quotation?

_____

_____

_____

_____

_____

2. How does the quotation beginning "There was ... " illustrate Henry's pre-battle thoughts about Nature?

_____

_____

_____

_____

_____

"moon . . . lighted" and "hung in a treetop," gives him solace (17). He soon learns that Nature is not that caring.

Deserting after his first moments in battle, Henry continues to read Nature as sympathetic to his plight. When he throws a pine cone at a squirrel, the squirrel scampers away, and Henry interprets the squirrel's escape as a sign that Nature approves of his own desertion: "She [Nature] re-enforced his argument with proofs that lived where the sun shone" (49). Only when he is wounded by a retreating soldier and returns with new determination to his duty does Henry realize that Nature's beauty stands separate from the black chaos and confusion of battle. After he participates in another fierce battle and witnesses its atrocities, he observes that the blue sky and the bright sun remain unaffected by the dark smoke and smoldering ruins below (105).

Constant and beautiful, Nature once again offers solace to the war-ravaged youth; however, he now sees Nature differently. Henry, as a seasoned veteran, looks at the sky, not for sympathy or justification for his actions, but in appreciation of the very indifference Nature has shown to the nightmare of battle:

> He turned now with a lover's thirst to images of tranquil skies, fresh meadows, cool brooks—an existence of soft and eternal peace.
>
> Over the river a golden ray of sun came through the hosts of leaden rain clouds. (143)

Having tested himself in battle, witnessed its terror and folly, and felt its grief, Henry looks to the constancy and beauty of Nature, which unfolds regardless of the actions of humanity.

3. How does the paraphrase beginning "After he participates …" support the main idea?

_____

_____

_____

_____

_____

4. How does the quotation beginning "He turned …" define Nature?

_____

_____

_____

_____

5. How does the writer's elaboration support the last quotation?

_____

_____

_____

_____

_____

DIRECTIONS Use ideas and information from the first paragraph of the passage you have just read to complete the graphic organizer.

Analyzing Literary Evidence

▶ PARAGRAPH 1 (From "'Here they come!'" to "eminently beautiful Nature.")	
Main Idea	
1. Introduction (how the main idea is supported in the introduction to the quotation)	*Henry is involved in a Civil War battle. Afterward, he looks up to the sky to get his bearings.*
2. Literary Evidence (how the main idea is supported by the quotation)	
3. Elaboration (how the quotation is tied back to the main idea)	

Writing Workshop: Literary Analysis of a Novel

DIRECTIONS Use the following guidelines to help you revise and correct the literary analysis on the next page.

THE INTRODUCTION SHOULD

- include the author's name, the title of the literary work, and relevant details about the author or work

- note relevant background information

- include a clear thesis that identifies the main point of the analysis

---

THE BODY SHOULD

- support and elaborate on the major points of the thesis

- include literary evidence from the text and/or secondary sources to support each major point

- effectively organize the main points of the paper and the literary evidence

---

THE CONCLUSION SHOULD

- restate the thesis

- summarize the main points of the analysis and bring it to a close

---

REMEMBER TO

❏ weave quotations into the structure of a given sentence

❏ introduce each quotation

❏ use literary present

Writing Workshop: Revising and Proofreading

DIRECTIONS The following literary analysis was written in response to this prompt:

> **Choose a character from a novel to analyze. Using specific references, identify the character's flaw and explain how it interferes with the character's relationships and impedes the character's development.**

The essay contains problems in content, style, organization, and usage.

- Use the space between the lines to revise the essay and correct the errors.
- If you cannot fit some of your revisions between the lines, rewrite the revised sections on a separate piece of paper.

Blinded by Jealousy

Set in Cold Sassy, Georgia, at the turn of the twentieth century, Olive Ann Burns's book tells the story of one year in the life of the narrator, Will Tweedy. The novel shows the changes in the attitudes of Will Tweedy as he grows closer to adulthood. Despite the coming-of-age theme in the book, the fourteen-year-old narrator allows his insecurities to blind him to the hardships of another teenage boy named Hosie Roach.

> **a.** Problem with introduction

Will's character flaws—insecurity and self-centeredness—keep him from seeing that while he is a privileged town boy who will inherit wealth, Hosie is a poor mill boy who must work to make something of himself. Will's father and grandfather are pleased with Hosie's work as soon as Hosie begins. Hosie scrubs himself clean and even shaves his head so that customers won't "git the nits"

> **b.** Problem with paragraph order

(345). Will misguidedly comments: "I really resented him wanting to please all that bad" (345).

At first, Will's insecurities make him suspicious of Hosie. When Will's grandfather says that he might offer Hosie a job in his store, Will reacts with spite and jealousy. He suggested to his grandfather that Hosie was not intelligent. Then, he tries to persuade his grandfather that Hosie is not fit to work in the store, stating that "he's got cooties and the itch and he stinks" (343).

c. Problem with literary present

Will is also unable to empathize with Hosie. The book says,

> Whereas I always had to go home in time to milk and
> bring in stovewood, he could stay all night if Grandpa
> wanted him to. And whereas my daddy always asked how
> much Latin or geometry I had to do that night, and lots of
> times made me go home early to get at it, Hosie would of
> course quit school if he got the job. (343–344)

d. Problem with introduction to quotation

Will does not take into consideration that Hosie does not have fresh milk, a fire at home, or a father who recognizes the importance of education.

Cold Sassy Tree is a good novel to read in high school, because it is about teenagers and it deals with things teenagers understand.

e. Problem with conclusion

Reading Workshop: An Article About History

DIRECTIONS Read the following passage, and answer the questions in the right-hand column.

America's Legacy from the Iroquois League

In 1991, Oren Lyons, chief of the Onondaga nation and a professor at the State University of New York at Buffalo, discussed in an interview the upsurge of American-inspired democracy throughout the world. He said, "But America got it from the Indians. America got the ideas of democracy and freedom and peace here."

Like Lyons, many people believe that American Indians, particularly the Iroquois, influenced the colonists who founded the United States. In 1988, a joint Congressional resolution stated that the U.S. "was influenced by the political system developed by the Iroquois Confederacy as were many of the democratic principles which were incorporated into the Constitution itself." Despite the resolution, many people are not familiar with the Iroquois Confederacy and the parallels between it and the U.S. government.

The Iroquois Confederacy, also known as the League of Five Nations, originated more than four hundred years ago. The League created an unwritten but detailed Great Law of Peace, or constitution, that was passed down through the generations. In 1900, the chiefs of the League approved an official written version of the constitution. This constitution authorized a council of fifty *sachems*, or chiefs, to make official decisions about affairs among member nations.

An obvious parallel between the League and the U.S. government is union itself. In *The Ambiguous Iroquois Empire*, author Francis Jennings states that the League was a confederation of nations related by language and culture, but with a history of being

1. After reading the first paragraph, what conclusion can you draw about the subjects the writer will compare in this article?

_____

_____

_____

_____

_____

2. What evidence does the writer use to establish a connection between the Iroquois and the colonists?

_____

_____

_____

_____

_____

3. Are the sources mentioned in the third and fourth paragraphs primary or secondary? Explain.

_____

_____

_____

_____

_____

separate. The thirteen American colonies were likewise united and sometimes at odds.

The League dealt only with issues concerning all the nations, primarily matters involving safety and defense. Merwyn Garbarino, author of *Native American Heritage,* states, "The League had nothing to do with internal affairs within each of the five tribes, but dealt with intertribal, external problems." Similarly, the U.S. Constitution spells out the powers delegated to the federal government, including national defense, reserving all other powers to state governments.

Both the League and the U.S. government established a representative government of delegates, and historians have noted similarities between League and Congressional procedures. In *Forgotten Founders*, historian Bruce Johansen states that the Great Law of Peace spelled out a "complex system of checks and balances." Negotiation was highly structured and consisted of a "two-house congress." The Onondagas filled an executive role and had veto power over other tribes. On an Internet site about the League, Richard Hooker notes that, like members of Congress, sachems conducted lengthy deliberations designed to overcome disputes. Like the U.S. Constitution, the Great Law of Peace also provided a mechanism for amending laws. Furthermore, as Johansen observes, "[T]he adoption laws of the confederacy . . . contained no bars on the basis of race or national origin."

Although few Americans may be aware of the principles on which the League was based, this was not the case with our nation's founders. The principles—characterized by Donald Grinde and Bruce Johansen in *Exemplar of Liberty* as "peace, brotherhood, and unity, a balance of power, the natural rights of all people, and sharing of resources"—are a part of the legacy of all Americans.

4. In the sixth paragraph, what types of sources does the writer use?

_____
_____
_____
_____

5. What information illustrates the similarity between League and Congressional procedures?

_____
_____
_____
_____

DIRECTIONS Use the ideas and information in the passage you have just read to complete the graphic organizer.

Drawing Conclusions

▶ **THE WRITER'S CONCLUSION:**

_____

Evidence cited to support the conclusion:

- ▪
- ▪
- ▪
- ▪
- ▪

▶ **YOUR CONCLUSION ABOUT THE ARTICLE'S RELIABILITY:**

_____

Your Reasons:

Writing Workshop: Historical Research Paper

DIRECTIONS Use the following guidelines to help you revise and correct the essay on the next page.

THE INTRODUCTION SHOULD

- draw readers into the research with an interesting opener
- give an overview of the research
- state the thesis

THE BODY SHOULD

- develop the thesis with several main ideas
- support ideas with factual information
- state some source material in the writer's own words
- credit sources, when necessary, in MLA format
- present ideas in an order that makes sense

THE CONCLUSION SHOULD

- restate the thesis
- provide a final assessment of the ideas

REMEMBER TO

- ❏ vary sentence beginnings
- ❏ punctuate citations correctly

Writing Workshop: Revising and Proofreading

DIRECTIONS The following research paper was written in response
to this prompt:

> **Write a research paper about a historical figure whose contribu-
> tions/actions were beneficial to society.**

The essay contains problems in style and content.

- Use the space between the lines to revise the style and correct the
  errors.
- If you cannot fit some of your revisions between the lines, rewrite
  the revised sections on a separate piece of paper.

A King for Ireland

Brian Boru reigned for almost forty years as one of Ireland's

greatest kings, first as King of Munster (present-day County Clare),

then as King of Ireland.

Between 976 and 978, Brian gained control over the Southern ter-

ritory of Munster (Duffy 26). At this time, Munster was Ireland's

largest province, and from 978 to 997, Brian attempted to maintain

control of the large territory. As king of Munster, he "consolidated

his strength, subdued his enemies, and made strong inroads on the

territory of the Ui Neill," whose king, Mael Sechnaill, claimed the

kingship of all of Ireland (Scherman 218).

By the year 1002, Mael Sechnaill acknowledged Brian's strength

and yielded his high kingship to Brian (Moody and Martin 113). For

the first time, all of the smaller kingships and territories in Ireland

were united under one king and one government.

a. Problem with
   thesis

During the twelve years of Brian's reign, Ireland enjoyed relative

peace and Brian solidified his position as king of all of Ireland. He

also began to rehabilitate schools and religious institutions and

rebuild the bridges and roads destroyed by Norse invaders (Moody

and Martin 113). As a result, Brian was "the first king who gave

Ireland something like a national consciousness" (Scherman 219).

Mael Sechnaill asked Brian for help. He did this when Norse

b. Problem with sentence beginnings

rebels refused to submit to him in 1014. The Irish, led by Brian and

his eldest son, defeated the Norse at the Battle of Clontarf, but both

Brian and his son were killed (Moody and Martin 115). Ireland was

never again united under one Irish king as cohesively as it had been

under Brian (Duffy 26).

From 1002 to 1014, Ireland enjoyed a relatively peaceful and

c. Problem with conclusion

prosperous period under one ruler.

Works Cited

Duffy, Seán, ed. <u>Atlas of Irish History</u>. New York: Macmillan USA,

1997.

Moody, T.W., and F.X. Martin, eds. <u>The Course of Irish History.</u>

Niwat, Colorado: Roberts Rinehart Publishers, 2001.

Scherman, Katharine. <u>The Flowering of Ireland: Saints, Scholars, and</u>

<u>Kings</u>. New York: Barnes and Noble, 1981.

for **CHAPTER 27**   *page 820*   **TEST**

Reading Workshop: Editorial

DIRECTIONS   Read the following passage, and answer the questions in the right-hand column.

Combating Road Rudeness

Drivers often use cars as weapons. Even considerate people can become impatient and dangerous drivers. We need to slow down and practice common courtesy every time we get behind the steering wheel of a car. Courtesy promotes safety and cooperation, something missing on today's roadways.

Impatient motorists frequently violate the rules of common courtesy. It is commonplace to see drivers passing on the right, blocking intersections, speeding outrageously, rapidly cutting in and out of traffic, tailgating, and failing to use turn signals. This kind of driving is not only rude, it is dangerous. According to the head of the National Highway Traffic Safety Administration, behaviors such as weaving in and out of traffic and running red lights are associated with about one-third of auto accidents. Frederik R. Mottola, executive director of the National Institute for Driver Behavior, suggests that drivers who tailgate are at a greater risk for crashes, while those who practice common courtesy and leave four seconds of following time between themselves and other drivers have "enough time to avoid a high-stress, high-risk crash."

Driving courteously also inspires others to respond in kind. Rude, aggressive behavior, on the other hand, causes others to become defensive and even go so far as to try to block another driver's progress. Think about it. How do you feel when someone refuses to let you merge onto a crowded freeway? Are you more or less likely to go out of your way to allow that driver to pass you later on? Driving diplomatically is the right thing to do, and once

1. How does the writer's use of "we" throughout the essay help gain the reader's trust?

_____

_____

_____

_____

2. What words and phrases in the second paragraph show the writer's bias?

_____

_____

_____

_____

_____

3. What kind of appeal does the quotation by Mr. Mottola demonstrate?

_____

_____

_____

_____

_____

you do it, you may be surprised at how often other drivers go out of their way to be helpful in return.

It is clear that we need a complete overhaul of our driving behaviors. We can start by thinking in terms of how our behavior behind the wheel affects other drivers. The thoughtful combination of courtesy and respect for others' safety sets a high standard of driving behavior that, with a little effort, all drivers can achieve.

4. What reason for driving courteously does the writer give in the third paragraph?

_____

_____

_____

_____

_____

5. What is the writer's overall point of view?

_____

_____

_____

_____

_____

DIRECTIONS Use the ideas and information in the editorial you have just read to complete the graphic organizer. Identify one example from the editorial of each type of appeal.

Identifying Persuasive Appeals

Logical Appeal

Emotional Appeal

Ethical Appeal

Writing Workshop: Editorial

DIRECTIONS Use the following guidelines to help you revise and correct the essay on the next page.

THE INTRODUCTION SHOULD

- grab the audience's attention
- give necessary background information
- contain a clear opinion statement

THE BODY SHOULD

- give convincing reasons and concrete evidence
- include strong logical, emotional, and ethical appeals with elaboration
- organize the appeals to reflect a logical progression of ideas
- include a rebuttal

THE CONCLUSION SHOULD

- restate the thesis
- give a call to action, if necessary

REMEMBER TO

- ❏ avoid euphemisms
- ❏ correct inexact pronoun references

Writing Workshop: Revising and Proofreading

DIRECTIONS The following editorial was written in response to this prompt:

> **Write an editorial concerning an issue that affects people your age.**

The editorial contains problems in content, style, and grammar.

- Use the space between the lines to revise the editorial and correct the errors.
- If you cannot fit some of your revisions between the lines, rewrite the revised sections on a separate piece of paper.

Wake-Up Call for Teen Fatigue

Medical research shows that adolescents need more sleep than

adults because sleep patterns of adolescents and adults differ.

> **a.** Problem with opening

> **b.** Problem with opinion statement

According to a report by Stanford University, teenagers need to

sleep nine hours and fifteen minutes every night. Teenagers rarely

get as much sleep as they need because schools start too early in the

morning. Instead of changing the school start time for students,

> **c.** Problem with inexact pronoun reference

administrators could suggest that they go to bed earlier to allow for

their particular sleep needs. However, many teenagers who go to

bed early lie awake for hours with insomnia. Teenagers, like every-

one else, have an internal biological clock, called circadian rhythms,

that determines when they can fall asleep. Unlike people of other

age groups, most teenagers' circadian rhythms program them to

stay up late at night and wake up late in the morning. Students can

make changes in their lives to help them sleep—such as going to

bed at the same time every night, avoiding caffeine, and dimming bright indoor lights at night—but, on the whole, circadian rhythms

are extremely difficult to change.

Scheduling high school classes to begin at 8:30 A.M. or later

makes sense because sleep deprivation can cause potentially serious

problems for teens when they drive to school.

> **d.** Problem with elabora-tion of evidence

Sleep deprivation can also interfere with learning. Tired students

have more memory problems and perform worse on tests than do

rested students. Moreover, learning stops when students cease to be

> **e.** Problem with euphemism

awake in class. Although starting school at a later hour does not

guarantee that students will make better grades, it does provide stu-

dents with the opportunity to arrive at school more

rested and alert.

Clearly, starting high school classes any earlier than 8:30 A.M. is a

losing proposition for teenagers. Holding classes when students

need to be asleep keeps students from getting the sleep they need

for good mental and physical health and can even be dangerous.

Reading Workshop: Book Review

DIRECTIONS Read the following passage, and answer the questions in the right-hand column.

Terror at the Top of the World

In March 1996, Jon Krakauer went to Nepal to accompany a commercial climbing crew to the top of Mount Everest. An avid climber for more than thirty years, Krakauer knew Everest's history and the risks involved. Little did he know, however, that he would be one of only two members on his team to reach the summit and come back alive. On May 10, 1996, a fierce storm trapped climbers from several competing climbing crews between their camp and the mountaintop, killing several and maiming others. The book *Into Thin Air* is Krakauer's gripping account of the ascent and his effort to set the record straight. He tries to explain what went wrong on Mount Everest that day and who was responsible for the resulting disaster. He successfully describes the awe that mountain climbing inspires and the awful consequences that result when humans miscalculate at the top of the world.

Krakauer vividly describes the tremendous physical and emotional challenges of each phase of the climb. He weaves vivid descriptions with quotations from his companions that seem poignantly ironic in light of the trip's outcome. For instance, guide Rob Hall repeatedly wonders which members of his climbing team he will need to rescue on this trip, never suspecting that he himself will perish.

Krakauer provides readers with a brief history of the modern fascination with Everest. He explains the important role of the Sherpas, a Tibetan people who have assisted climbers to the top of Everest since 1921. Any potentially confusing material is clarified in footnotes. Detailed lists tell readers what teams were on the mountain

1. Why does the reviewer begin with this background information?

_____

_____

_____

_____

2. In the first paragraph, what clue words signal the writer's opinion of the book?

_____

_____

_____

_____

_____

3. In the third paragraph, what criterion for evaluation does the reviewer establish?

_____

_____

_____

_____

_____

that spring, and maps show where victims were trapped. Krakauer's inclusion of these materials enables readers to navigate through the complicated series of events.

    Finally, Krakauer thoroughly reconstructs the events of May 10. Acknowledging the effects that altitude had upon his own perception and memory, Krakauer interviewed other survivors of the disaster to see if their memories corroborated his own. The record of the day's events is also supported by his research into the radio log books of the base camp. *Into Thin Air* remains primarily a first-person recollection; however, Krakauer avoids oversimplifying what went wrong on the mountain. He refuses to place blame squarely on anyone's shoulders and, instead, chronicles the series of actions and behaviors of the climbing crews that played a role in the outcome. Although he suggests that oxygen deprivation and business rivalry might have led some of the guides to make unwise choices, he depicts the primary culprits as the unpredictable weather and the extremely harsh environment on Mount Everest.

    By trying to understand what went wrong, Jon Krakauer seems to be dealing with the loss of his friends and his own vulnerability. *Into Thin Air* provokes sympathy for the victims and their families and shows that even in an age when Everest has been conquered, the mountain remains unpredictable and worthy of our respect.

4. What evidence does the writer use to support the opinion that Krakauer thoroughly reconstructs the events of May 10?

_____

_____

_____

_____

_____

5. In the conclusion, what additional reasons does the reviewer offer to support a positive or negative opinion of the book?

_____

_____

_____

_____

_____

DIRECTIONS Use the criteria provided by the reviewer in the passage you have just read to complete the graphic organizer.

Identifying Criteria for Evaluation

CRITERION	REVIEWER'S JUDGMENT	EVIDENCE FROM REVIEW
	Yes ☐ No ☐ Explanation:	
	Yes ☐ No ☐ Explanation:	*history of Mount Everest's exploration; who the Sherpas are; footnotes and maps*
The information in the book is accurate and is drawn from a number of personal accounts and authoritative sources.	Yes ☐ No ☐ Explanation:	

Writing Workshop: Book Review

DIRECTIONS Use the following guidelines to help you revise and correct the review on the next page.

THE INTRODUCTION SHOULD

- hook the readers and make them want to read the review
- provide background information to help readers understand the review
- provide a brief summary of the book
- state a clear and assertive opinion that includes the topic and main idea of the review

THE BODY SHOULD

- support the opinion statement with three or more reasons and evidence
- logically organize reasons and evidence

THE CONCLUSION SHOULD

- restate the opinion
- leave the readers with something to think about

REMEMBER TO

- ❑ use precise and meaningful adjectives
- ❑ punctuate quotations correctly

Writing Workshop: Revising and Proofreading

DIRECTIONS The following book review was written in response to this prompt:

Review a nonfiction book. Establish clear criteria for evaluation, and support your opinions.

The review contains problems in style, content, and mechanics.

- Use the space between the lines to revise the review and correct the errors.
- If you cannot fit some of your revisions between the lines, rewrite the revised sections on a separate piece of paper.

Life as a Lad in Limerick

What could be worse than growing up in America during the Great Depression? If you ask Frank McCourt, he might answer, "Growing up in extreme poverty in Ireland." Frank McCourt is a retired public-school teacher born in New York at the beginning of the Great Depression. His alcoholic father and struggling mother decided to move the family back to Limerick, Ireland, when McCourt was four, only to find that their move did not improve their desperate circumstances. *Angela's Ashes* is McCourt's best-selling memoir of growing up in extreme poverty, first in New York and then in Ireland, where he lived until he was nineteen. I think *Angela's Ashes* is a truly excellent book.

> **a.** Problem with opinion statement

Although *Angela's Ashes* presents a sad picture of McCourt's childhood, its tone is not self-pitying. McCourt describes the sad actions of adults in great detail, but he balances those descriptions with humor and affection. He notes that the family's financial prob-lems were caused by his father's drinking, but the overall picture of

> **b.** Problem with adjectives

his father is tenderly drawn. In short, unlike many stories of a diffi-

cult childhood, *Angela's Ashes* has a loving and forgiving tone.

McCourt's marvelous writing style also makes this book a joy to

read. Run-on sentences like this one perfectly capture the thought

and speech patterns of a child:

> Mam wets an old towel and scrubs my face till it stings, she
>
> wraps the towel around her finger and sticks it in my ears and
>
> claims there's enough wax there to grow potatoes . . . she tells
>
> me to shut up and stop the whinging.

c. Problem with omitted words in quotation

In addition, vivid details and dialogue bring the story and the

characters to life. For example, McCourt's description of the family's

tiny house, with the lavatory for the whole lane outside the front

door, the "lake in the kitchen" when the River Shannon floods, and

the ever-present dampness, allows the reader to "see" the miserable

poverty of McCourt's childhood. Conversations with family mem-

bers, teachers, and social workers are recounted word-for-word,

making the memoir come alive for the reader.

Angela's Ashes is a great book. Any reader who enters McCourt's

world will discover that even a cold and wet Ireland could not

dampen a child's spirit.

d. Problem with restate- ment of opinion

Reading Workshop: Critique of Advertising

DIRECTIONS Read the following passage, and answer the questions in the right-hand column.

A Powerful Message from a Drug-Free Dynamo

There she is, one of the brightest lights in tennis, her face framed with beads as she smiles broadly. Wearing court clothes and carrying a racquet, she looks relaxed and confident. Her photograph is superimposed on a round, green object—perhaps a planet, or perhaps a tennis ball. Is this an advertisement for one of Venus Williams's upcoming matches? You might think so—until you read the slogan: "There are no drugs on Planet Venus." This ad, sponsored by the Office of National Drug Control Policy, appeared in a fashion magazine for girls. The ad provides no statistics, but it still effectively conveys the message that smart young people should avoid drugs.

The text of the ad pulls readers in with a clever play on Venus Williams's name, then uses repetition to reinforce the message. The red "no drugs" in the slogan is echoed by five *nos* in the copy.

The *no* statements remind readers of the obvious dangers of a drug habit and the joys of clean living. The first two statements describe the negatives that can be avoided by saying no: "No burned-out dreams gone up in smoke" and "No looking stupid, feeling like a loser, or hurting the family because of drugs." The next two statements describe the good things that those who avoid drugs can expect: "No problem finding better things to do" and "No shortage of cool people to do better things with." The last line of the copy refers back to the confident, athletic Williams: "No doubt, intelligent life exists here."

1. What is the writer's opinion about the advertisement?

_____

_____

_____

_____

_____

2. What evidence does the writer give to support the idea that the text of the ad is effective?

_____

_____

_____

_____

_____

But who is the subject of the compelling statements? No English teacher would allow these sentence fragments to stand, but the ad uses ambiguity by leaving out the subject. Is it Venus Williams who is saying *no*? Is it you, the reader? This ambiguity is the heart of the ad's persuasive message: It applies to both Venus and the reader; by avoiding drugs, the ad says, anyone can be like Venus.

The ad's composition—the way colors, shapes, lines, and textures are used—also enhances its persuasive punch. In a red shirt, Williams stands out boldly against a green and black background— she is someone who stands out from the crowd. The words "no drugs" circle her in red to match her shirt, reinforcing the association between Williams and the anti-drug message.

Even though many readers will not pause long enough to notice the ad's clever language or consider its visual punch, these readers will see Venus Williams and the words "no drugs." In essence, this ad is a simple testimonial, associating the desirable attributes of a famous person with a persuasive message. The ad does not need to spell out the message. Williams's beaming face tells the reader that joy, health, confidence, athletic ability, and success are incompatible with drug use.

The lack of statistics on drug use does not detract from the ad's effectiveness. The perils of drug use are well known. Many ads have used scare tactics to convince young people. This ad gives readers something positive to reach for: the health, confidence, and power embodied in Venus Williams.

3. According to the writer, why is Venus Williams an effective spokesperson?

_____
_____
_____
_____
_____

4. Based on your prior experience, do you think that testimonials are an effective advertising device? Explain.

_____
_____
_____
_____

5. Do you agree that statistics are not needed to make this advertisement effective? Explain.

_____
_____
_____
_____

Advertisement "There are no drugs on Planet Venus" from *Seventeen Magazine*, November 1999. Copyright © 1999 by ***Partnership for a Drug Free America***. Reprinted by permission of the copyright holder.

DIRECTIONS To complete the graphic organizer, use the ideas and information in the passage you have just read.

Analyzing Emotional Appeals

▶ QUOTATIONS	▶ ANALYSIS OF EMOTIONAL APPEALS
"The *no* statements remind readers of the obvious dangers of a drug habit and the joys of clean living."	*makes me think that everyone knows drugs are bad and that life without drugs is great*

Here's how these quotations play on my emotions:

REVISING GUIDELINES

Writing Workshop: Evaluating an Advertisement

DIRECTIONS Use the following guidelines to help you revise and correct the evaluation on the next page.

THE INTRODUCTION SHOULD

- contain an attention-grabber

- describe the ad, give background information, and state the target audience

- contain a two-part thesis stating the ad's persuasiveness and evaluating the ad's potential effect on people

THE BODY SHOULD

- discuss one criterion in each section

- have effectively organized sections

- contain evidence and examples from the ad

- explain the persuasive techniques used in the ad

THE CONCLUSION SHOULD

- sum up the thesis

- make a judgment about the ad's potential effect on people

REMEMBER TO

❏ eliminate unnecessary passive-voice *be* verbs

❏ correct sentence fragments

ELEMENTS OF LANGUAGE | Fifth Course

Writing Workshop: Revising and Proofreading

DIRECTIONS The following evaluation of an advertisement was
written in response to this prompt:

> **Write an evaluation of an advertisement. Your thesis should
> evaluate how persuasive the ad is and whether it is fair, accurate,
> or beneficial to consumers.**

The evaluation contains problems in style, organization, usage, and
mechanics.

- Use the space between the lines to revise the evaluation and correct the errors.
- If you cannot fit some of your revisions between the lines, rewrite
  the revised sections on a separate sheet of paper.

Happiness for Sale, Caribbean Style

An ad for Barbados, with a picture of a woman dancing in a

brightly colored costume, appeared in a travel magazine. The ad's

copy asks, "When was the last time you celebrated absolutely noth-

ing but the pure joy of being alive?" The ad says that a vacation in

Barbados would be pleasurable and exciting.

> **a.** Problem with thesis

The ad uses repetition to convey its message. The repeated forms

of the word "joy" in the ad's copy and in the large banner across the

bottom work with the image of the laughing woman to imply that

Barbados can provide the happiest vacation ever.

Although repetition, association, and composition successfully

work together to make this ad effective, the persuasiveness really

hinges on one misleading technique: omission. The accommoda-

tions and travel costs to Barbados can accumulate into the thou-

sands and, clearly, were purposely omitted.

> **b.** Problem with paragraph
> order

Many of the details in this ad are symbolic; they evoke pleasant images readers associate with an island vacation. For instance, the orange and yellow flowers in the woman's costume summon images of tropical flowers tourists might see on this island. Similarly, the soft glow from the windows in the background resembles candlelight. A feature that many readers will associate with romance. Finally, the banner appears in the bright gold color of a tropical sun. The ad plays into many positive associations. That readers may have about island vacations.

> **c.** Problems with sentence fragments

One of the most interesting ways this ad persuades is through composition. The design is emphasizing motion. The outline of the dancer's turban and skirts is indistinct; she is surrounded by a soft orange blur, as if she has just turned her head and has flipped her skirt rapidly.

> **d.** Problem with unnecessary *be* verbs

The purpose of this ad is to create a compelling image of Barbados for prospective tourists. Through repetition, association, composition, and omission. The ad achieves that goal, but it does not do so fairly. The ad reinforces the notion that in order to be happy, people need to take an exotic vacation. It is not fair of the tourism industry to tap into people's desire to escape.

> **e.** Problem with sentence fragment